To
Cecil Burney
— who also had
a role in the events
that shaped this book.
With best regards
Booth Mooney

The

Lyndon B. Johnson

PRESIDENTIAL COLLECTION

of

Mr. and Mrs. Cecil E. Burney

MR. SPEAKER

Four Men Who Shaped the

United States House of Representatives

HENRY CLAY   JOSEPH G. CANNON

THOMAS B. REED   SAM RAYBURN

Mr. Speaker

FOUR MEN WHO SHAPED THE

UNITED STATES

HOUSE OF REPRESENTATIVES

by Booth Mooney

1964

Follett Publishing Company

Chicago

Manufactured in the United States of America

Designed by Gordon Martin

FOLLETT PUBLISHING COMPANY
1000 West Washington Boulevard
Chicago, Illinois 60607

This book is for

BETTY

CONTENTS

AUTHOR'S PREFACE

One day when I was trying to persuade the late Speaker Sam Rayburn, who extended his friendship to me during the last decade of his life, to cooperate with me in the writing of a book about his career in the House of Representatives, he returned his usual blunt but kind and regretful refusal and then countered with a suggestion of his own: instead of doing a book about him alone, I should devote myself to a study of several of the outstanding Speakers of the House and write a book about them.

As he expanded on this idea, Mr. Rayburn became increasingly enthusiastic. It was a great subject, he declared, for anyone interested in how government really worked. As he proceeded, I dismissed the suspicious thought that he was simply trying to keep me from badgering him further. He meant exactly what he was saying, and as usual, he was sincere with his offer to help. He sat down to make up a list of the Speakers who should be part of the book. And he volunteered that—if I wished him to—he would even write a foreword for the book.

The list of Speakers he suggested contained the names of several in addition to those I have treated at length in the pages that follow. It included four with whom he had served in the House: Champ Clark, Nicholas Longworth, William B. Bankhead, and John Nance Garner. He also advised that consideration should be given to James G. Blaine and to Samuel J. Randall. In this conversation and others that followed, we eventually agreed that any listing of Speakers who had done most to shape the House of Representatives would have to include—no matter who else was omitted—Henry Clay, Thomas B. Reed, Joseph G. Cannon, and Sam Rayburn ("if only because I've been around so long and so much has happened," he said matter-of-factly). It is these four whose stories are told in this book.

In the notes from my talks with Mr. Rayburn about the foreword he promised to write, I have this statement from him: "My own feeling is that every one of the thousands of men and women who has held House membership has had an individual share—maybe big, maybe little—in molding the House and making it what it is." That was, of course, an expression of how he felt about the institution with which he had been identified for so long. He would have been content, I think, if I had decided in the end to write an encyclopedic biography of *all* the men who had occupied the Speaker's chair in the House. He himself would probably have found some charitable things to say about each of them.

In any event, I emphasize that the choices in this volume are mine. There have been other great Speakers in addition to Henry Clay, Thomas B. Reed, Joseph G. Cannon, and Sam Rayburn, but it is my opinion that these are the men who, more than any others, influenced the structure and direction of the House of Representatives.

These four were about as different as men can be one from another. This is not surprising, however, for through many years it has been demonstrated that the House itself is not always the same institution. These four Speakers were quite aware of that. It was part of their political genius that they conducted themselves in accordance with the knowledge that the House could change, and change suddenly.

Turning again to my notes of the conversations with Mr. Rayburn about his foreword (I became engaged with other matters and postponed writing the book until it was forever too late to get that foreword), I find, also in his words, "The House has been a constantly changing body throughout its history. That is natural. The problems and needs and wants of the people are always in a state of change. The result is a continual shift, evidenced every two years, in the membership of the House. That is how the House is kept representative of the people."

The power and the influence of the speakership have varied greatly, too, for not all the men who have held the position wished to gain power, or were able to gain power, and use it in the fashion of Clay, Reed, Cannon, and Rayburn, under the leadership of each of whom, the House of Representatives exercised its constitutional role in the United States government with full strength.

At other times, and for diverse reasons, the Senate has been the predominant chamber, or the Executive has overshadowed both houses of the Congress. However, that was not the case when any one of these four men was the Speaker of the House. They understood how to manage men and legislation, and as a result of their efforts the House of Representatives knew days and years of power and glory.

Booth Mooney
Washington, 1964

ON THE PRINCIPLES

REGULATING THE SPEAKER'S DUTIES

[The principles] enjoin promptitude and impartiality in deciding the various questions of order as they arise; firmness and dignity in his deportment toward the House; patience, good temper, and courtesy toward the individual members; and the best arrangement and distribution of the talent of the House, in its numerous subdivisions, for the dispatch of the public business; and the fair exhibition of every subject presented for consideration. They especially require of him, in those moments of agitation from which no deliberative assembly is always entirely exempt, to remain cool and unshaken amidst all the storms of debate, carefully guarding the preservation of the permanent laws and rules of the House from being sacrificed to temporary passions, prejudices, or interests.

HENRY CLAY
December 1, 1823, on being
elected Speaker for the
sixth time

I

The Speaker

THE SPEAKER of the United States House of Representatives, said Thomas Brackett Reed, who once held the position, "has but one superior and no peer." Other men, including other Speakers, have contended that the individual holding the speakership is only first among equals in the House. In either case, it is certain that during the evolution of the "popular branch" of the American Congress whenever a strong and able man has been Speaker he has wielded tremendous power, second only to that of the President of the nation.

This power is so great that it cannot be precisely measured; at the same time it is so unstructured that it cannot be precisely defined. The power emanates from various sources. The Speaker is the elected representative of the people's representatives. In being named to the speakership he may be said to have received, indirectly, a majority of the votes of all the people of the United States. Since he is a symbol of the House of Representatives, and since all tax bills must originate in the House, and since appropriation bills traditionally have originated there (subject, of course, to amendment in the Senate), the Speaker is warmly courted by department heads in the Executive branch.

The Speaker strongly influences, although he no longer completely controls, the appointment of House members to committees, which is a matter of considerable moment to ambitious politicians. Being in charge of the complex parliamentary machinery of the House, he can speed bills up or delay action on them and can foster floor debate or cut it off. He can refrain, if he so chooses, from seeing a member who is trying to gain recognition by the Chair. Even if he does admit to seeing him, the Speaker can ask, "For what purpose does the gentleman rise?" and if the answer is unsatisfactory his attention may wander elsewhere, leaving the member, as one once disconsolately complained, "silent, mute, and unheard."

The Speaker, along with the President and the Vice-President, must sign every piece of enacted legislation before it can become law. And the Speaker is next in line of succession after the Vice-President to succeed to the presidency of the United States.

Yet, while the command of the Speaker over the House of Representatives is indeed great, it is not all-prevailing. His rulings can be, and have been, overturned. Thus, finally, he governs, in the American tradition, by the consent of the governed. Nevertheless, so long as he uses his power in such a way as to retain the confidence of a majority of the membership, he is the final authority on everything in the House—from the procedure for operating the elevators of its office building to the course its legislative program will follow.

This was not always so, and there is no evidence that the framers of the Constitution meant it ever to be so.

1

The Constitution does provide that "The House of Representatives shall choose their Speaker and other officers," but has nothing to say about either his status or his duties. There is not even a provision that he must be a member of the House, although he always has been. A former House parliamentarian, Asher C. Hinds, thought that the framers of the Constitution did not create the speakership but simply adopted an existing office, the House Speaker thus being a direct descendant of the Speaker in the colonial assemblies.

"Mr. Speaker" of the House of Representatives today offers a sharp contrast to the Speaker of the English House of Commons, who, originally the "King's man" and later the majority floor leader, has been since 1839 the impartial umpire of that body. The English Speaker is elected by the members of Commons, subject to formal approval by the Crown. Upon election he ceases to be a politician, severs his former political affiliations, and becomes the presiding officer and the servant of the whole House. He does not inject himself into the work of committees. He attends no party caucuses. He makes no political speeches. He in fact gives up his rights as a constituency-representing member of Commons. His role is to preside over deliberations of the House, maintain order in debate, decide questions arising on points of order, put questions for decision, and declare the decisions.

The Speaker of the United States House of Representatives performs these functions, too, but he is not confined to them. He serves in a threefold capacity. He is the body's presiding officer, the political leader of the majority party in the House, and the representative of his home congressional district. As a member, he has the right to vote on all questions—unlike the Vice-President, who, as presiding officer of the Senate, has no vote except in the case of a tie. In modern times, the Speaker usually has not used his voting right except to break a tie or to make known for the record his stand on a particular measure. The Speaker also has the privilege of leaving the Chair and participating in debate on the House floor, which the Vice-President may not do in the Senate. Nowadays, advantage is but infrequently taken of this privilege; but when the Speaker does step down from the Chair to have his say, the House listens attentively.

The Speaker derives his parliamentary powers and duties from the Constitution, the rules of the House, precedents established by past decisions, and general parliamentary law. His political powers depend primarily upon his personality and ability and—as his service lengthens—upon his skill in cashing the political I O U's he has gathered by extending

3

favors to members of the House. The successful Speakers have been men who earned the confidence and respect not only of members of their own party but of the general membership of the House as well.

"The Speaker should be a man of strength," declared Sam Rayburn, who held the post longer than anyone else. "Naturally, any strong leader will use all the power that is given him or he can get."

That was not the concept in the beginning. The duties assigned to the Speaker by the first standing rule adopted by the First Congress in 1789 were modeled closely on those of the Speaker in the English House of Commons.

Frederick A. C. Muhlenberg, a Representative from Pennsylvania, was chosen Speaker of the first House by majority vote. There was not much for him to do beyond performing his functions as presiding officer. The House had only sixty-five members—fifty-five Federalists and ten Anti-Federalists—and thus was small enough for most major measures to be formulated by the entire membership sitting as a Committee of the Whole. There was no system of standing committees. All the principal legislation of the first few Congresses was hammered out in the Committee of the Whole and then referred to select committees, which worked out the details on particular bills and passed out of existence.

It immediately became evident, however, that certain legislative subjects, such as governmental revenue, appropriations, military affairs, and domestic commerce, would be before the House in session after session. So the House began to create standing committees, adding to them as new problems arose. The first was the Committee on Elections, created in 1789. The Committee on Claims was established in 1795, and by the end of the century standing committees had been formed for Interstate and Foreign Commerce and for Revisal and Unfinished Business.

During the nineteenth century, more and more select committees were turned into standing committees, and by 1900

4

the House had fifty-eight standing committees, with the number increasing still further during the early years of the twentieth century. In 1946, however, the committee structure was completely revised, and the number of standing committees was reduced to nineteen. One committee, that on Science and Astronautics, has been added since.

Political activity as it is today known and enthusiastically practiced in the House of Representatives could hardly be said to have existed in the early years. Even when it did commence, legislative control and leadership traced back to the President. The Chief Executive depended on his own power and the assistance of trusted floor lieutenants. The result was that during the first two decades of congressional history the Speakers of the House were merely figureheads. Leadership was conferred by the President, not by the House, and the floor leader was the man who had the President's ear. This was especially evident during the Jefferson Administration.

Inevitably this situation would change, if only because the man in the White House would not always be forceful enough to grasp and hold the reins of legislative leadership—the only leadership that really counts, according to a governmental theory later propounded by Woodrow Wilson (in *Congressional Leadership*, written in 1885). "In a country which governs itself by means of a public meeting, a Congress, or a parliament," Wilson stated, "the only real leadership in governmental affairs must be the legislative. . . . The leaders, if there be any, must be those who suggest the opinions and rule the actions of the legislative body." Accordingly, throughout the political history of the United States, there has been an incessant power struggle between the Executive and Legislative branches.

The first shift in the balance of power from the President to Congress came after Jefferson was succeeded by James Madison. Congress then began the development of its own leadership machinery and its own power system. This was due in part to the weakness of the new President in comparison

5

with the three men who had preceded him in office. Factional fights inside the Madison Cabinet also helped to create an atmosphere favorable to the success of the House rebellion against Executive control. The greatest force for change, however, was the emergence in the House of a group of young, energetic, and bellicose men led by Henry Clay, who became the new Speaker.

The young nation had entered a period of change. The changes were sharply reflected in the House of Representatives, where Clay and his dedicated young cohorts quickly demonstrated that they were in control. Clay added both power and prestige to the speakership. No longer was the Speaker merely chairman of the House, no longer was he inferior in influence to the floor leader as during the Jeffersonian regime. With Clay at the helm, the Speaker was the leader of the majority party as well as the presiding officer of the House. Further command was centered in the speakership with the fuller development of the standing committee system in 1816, followed by a change in the rules to provide for the appointment of committee chairmen by the Speaker.

Clay's concept of the speakership was openly partisan. It was a concept further developed by Andrew Stevenson, who was Speaker from 1827 to 1834, and James K. Polk, Speaker from 1835 to 1839, although they were not strong Speakers, as Clay was, since they were subservient to President Andrew Jackson. During the remainder of the nineteenth century the political power of the Speaker grew until it reached its peak between 1890 and 1910 under the velvet-clad iron hand of Speaker Thomas B. Reed and the mailed fist of Speaker Joseph G. Cannon.

2

Contests for the speakership have not occurred in modern years. The formal offering of a candidate by each of the two major political parties is made with the foreknowledge that the majority party in the House will name the Speaker. During the first half of the nineteenth century, however, it was not uncommon for the election of a Speaker to result in a contest or even a deep-seated conflict that lasted for days or weeks. The slavery issue was the principal factor in most of these disputes.

An election contest caused one of the most serious struggles over the election of a Speaker. This was in 1839. When the Congress convened on December 2 of that year, New Jersey sent two sets of representatives to Washington. One was Whig, one Democratic. Without the New Jersey membership the House had 119 Democrats and 118 Whigs, so admission of either of the contested delegations would give its party a majority. Future President Polk, Speaker in the previous session, was no longer in Congress and could not be called to act as interim chairman of the House. The House clerk refused to put any question to the membership, contending that he had no authority to do so. No one was in command.

Finally, after nearly two weeks of chaos, the House agreed that its most distinguished member, former President John Quincy Adams, should assume the Chair on a temporary basis. Under his guidance, an agreement was reached to take a vote for Speaker, with the two contesting delegations from New Jersey denied the right to participate. The Democrats, with a majority of one, had been holding out for just such a decision. But the delay had been too long. A few Democrats had become dissatisfied with the way things were going. These dissidents allied themselves with the Whigs and the combination chose for Speaker a thirty-year-old Virginian, Robert M. T. Hunter, who had become acceptable by declaring himself an Independent. Hunter had been in Congress only two years. He was the youngest man ever to be Speaker. Called by Adams "a good-hearted, weak-headed young man prematurely hoisted into a place for which he is not fit," he was not re-elected to the speakership in 1841.

One of the most acrimonious battles for the post took place

in 1849; it continued for three weeks and through sixty-three ballots. No party had a clear majority in the House that year, several Free-Soil Whigs and Democrats functioning as Independents. The issue in conflict was whether or not the district and territorial committees of the House were to have pro-slavery majorities. That would be determined by the identity of the Speaker, since he would appoint the committees. The two leading candidates for Speaker were Howell Cobb of Georgia, Democrat, and Robert C. Winthrop of Massachusetts, Whig. Winthrop had been Speaker of the House in the preceding Congress. When the first vote was taken December 3, 1849, there were eleven candidates in all. Cobb received 103 votes, eight short of a majority.

Voting continued daily until December 22. During that period sundry efforts were made to resolve the matter by changing the rules. After the thirtieth ballot a Representative offered a resolution that the speakership be filled by lottery, with one name from each of the five political factions to be placed in a box from which the clerk of the House would then draw a name. But the motion was tabled.

So were other motions: to elect a Speaker by a plurality instead of a majority; to name a Speaker and other House officers pro tempore; to provide that no member of the House should receive salary or mileage payment until a Speaker had been elected. On one desperate day, Andrew Johnson proposed that ministers of the gospel be invited to attend sessions and pray for an end to the disorganized state of the House. But the members could not agree even on this proposal, and it, too, was tabled.

It became gravely clear that a Speaker could not be elected by majority vote. At last, on December 22, 1849, the House for the first time in its history abandoned the principle of majority rule. Members agreed, by a vote of 113 to 106, that a Speaker could be elected by a plurality provided that it was a majority of a quorum (half the membership plus one) of the House. Cobb and Winthrop had alternated in the lead

through the long December days of voting. Now, on the final
test, Cobb received 102 votes out of 222, Winthrop 100, and
the remaining twenty votes were scattered among eight
other candidates. Cobb's election then was confirmed by a
majority vote.

An even more protracted fight occurred at the beginning of
the Thirty-fourth Congress in 1855. It went on for two months
and eventually was settled on the hundred and twenty-second
ballot after the House had resorted once more to election of
a Speaker by a plurality. The slavery issue again was at the
root of the conflict, but this time the outcome favored the
antislavery forces. Nathaniel P. Banks of Massachusetts was
chosen over William Aikin of South Carolina.

Another heated contest for the speakership came in the
Thirty-sixth Congress, which convened on the eve of the Civil
War. This struggle lasted from December 5, 1859, until
February 1, 1860, and resulted in the election of a compromise
candidate in the person of William Pennington, a former governor of New Jersey and a new member of the House. In the
voting for the speakership, his name appeared for the first time
on the thirty-eighth ballot when he received one vote. Not
until the weary forty-fourth ballot was he elected. Pennington
held the speakership in only that Congress. In fact, he held
his seat in the House in only that Congress, for he was defeated in his try for re-election.

After the Civil War, there were no more bitter and prolonged floor fights over the election of a Speaker. One cause
of the new peace was the removal of the slavery issue as a
source of contention. Perhaps of broader significance was the
establishment after the war of two more or less clearly defined
political parties, each of which developed its own mature and
experienced leadership.

A minor exception to the trend toward harmony in the
election of a Speaker may be noted in the case of the Sixty-
eighth Congress, which convened December 3, 1923. The
Republicans had a clear majority with 225 members in the

House, the remaining membership being composed of 205 Democrats, one Independent, one Farmer-Laborite, and one Socialist. Among the Republicans, however, were some twenty members who, calling themselves Progressives, presented their own candidate for Speaker as a protest against certain House rules. But Nicholas Longworth of Ohio, floor leader for the Republicans, worked out an agreement with this group, and the "regular" Republican candidate, Frederick H. Gillett of Massachusetts, was elected Speaker on the ninth roll call.

Since then, the speakership candidate of the majority party has been elected as a matter of course. The question of who is going to be Speaker is settled for all practical purposes in pre-session party caucus—that is, a meeting of all congressmen belonging to the same political party, usually held the day before a session begins. Even in the caucus the outcome is rarely in doubt.

3

The rules of the House are of fundamental importance to the man who sits in the Speaker's chair, for he derives a major portion of his parliamentary power from those rules. Under the Constitution each branch of Congress may determine the rules of its proceedings, and in practice the House of Representatives has done so at the beginning of each new Congress. Usually—although not always—the adoption of rules takes the form of acquiescing in those that prevailed in the sessions of the previous House.

A sweeping revision of House rules, which had grown by a process of accretion since 1789, was made in 1860. The revised rules were not found satisfactory for long. The principal objection to them was that they imposed too many restrictions on the liberty of the individual member by giving him insufficient opportunity to study legislative measures before they were submitted for House action. The dissatisfaction grew more pronounced with the increase in the size of the House and the volume of its business in the years after the Civil War.

In 1872 the House passed a resolution providing for the appointment of a committee to revise the rules, but no record exists of any report made by this committee. Another effort came in 1879, when the House named a committee of five members to sit during the congressional recess for the purpose of revising and simplifying the rules. The committee's unanimous report, adopted by the House as the general rules revision of 1880, laid the groundwork for the flow of dominating authority in that body into the hands of the Speaker.

The Rules Committee became a standing panel of five members, three from the majority and two from the minority. The committee could authorize suspension of the rules by a majority vote, limit debate, or completely block consideration of a bill. Speaker Samuel J. Randall, Pennsylvania Democrat, who was chairman of the first standing Committee on Rules, added to its power by requiring that it pass on all proposals to change the rules. Since the Speaker was chairman of this committee and could appoint his men to it, the man in the Chair could rule the House if he were strong enough.

If he were strong enough—and Thomas B. Reed of Maine was, as he demonstrated when he forced the adoption of the famous "Reed Rules" of 1890. Reed handed down two historic decisions. One was that a vote is valid if a quorum of the House is physically present, even though some members making up the quorum refuse to vote. The other was that obviously dilatory motions offered with the intent of obstructing the business of the House need not be entertained by the Speaker. These two decisions were incorporated in the new rule book which the House adopted on February 14, 1890, after much wrangling.

Reed also refined the power of the Speaker to deny recognition to a member. Even before the Civil War, Linn Boyd of Kentucky, the Speaker during 1851 and 1852, had stated that "the rules confer authority on the Chair to name the member entitled to the floor." James G. Blaine, during his speakership from 1869 to 1875, set up an informal censorship over motions and reports by demanding that members consult him in advance when they planned to seek recognition. For years it had been accepted that a member could appeal to the House if the Speaker refused to recognize him, but in 1881 Speaker Randall held that the right of recognition was as absolute in the Chair "as the judgment of the Supreme Court is in its interpretation of the law." Reed went further. He it was who established the precedent of asking, "For what purpose does the gentleman rise?" and then refusing recognition if he elected to do so.

Now, in truth, the Speaker was the boss of the House. He appointed all standing committees and designated their chairmen. He himself was chairman of the almost omnipotent Rules Committee and thus could determine what legislative business should come before the House. His unlimited power of recognition on the floor gave him additional means of disciplining the members.

The autocratic regime established by Reed held up for twenty years, varying in its stringency with different Speakers and reaching an apex of dictatorship under Cannon of Illinois. The majority party simply turned over its power in the House to one man. Any member who might entertain dreams of rebellion had to remember that the Speaker controlled his committee assignments and thus his political advancement. This was indeed the era in the House when members had to "go along to get along." The favors handed out by Cannon and his few close friends to Representatives who supported the bewhiskered, profane, and somewhat lovable old Speaker were rigidly withheld from active rebels.

Then there was a successful revolution—the House Revolution of 1910. Cannon's heavy-handed rule had gone on too long. Not only within the House itself but throughout the country, and notably in the press, a storm of opposition arose against the manner in which and the motives for which the powers of the speakership were being used. This festering discontent came to a head in 1910 when a coalition of rebellious

Republicans and Democrats, led by the Nebraska liberal, George W. Norris, conducted a successful assault on the rules that made the Speaker's tyranny possible.

When the struggle was over, the leadership system of the House had been drastically changed. No longer was the Speaker to serve as the chairman or even as a member of the vitally important Rules Committee. The committee was enlarged, and provisions were made for its members to be elected by the House and for the committee to name its own chairman. In addition, the Speaker was stripped of his power to appoint other standing committees and to designate their chairmen. Even his right of recognition from the Chair was restricted.

After the overthrow of Cannonism, a strong system of partisan government, based on the party caucus, was established in the House. Champ Clark, the amiable and able Missouri Democrat who succeeded Cannon to the speakership, followed a practice of bringing together the whole party membership in the House to make major decisions. In the early years of Clark's tenure this caucus was dominated not by the Speaker but by the majority floor leader. Under the new rules the majority leader was chairman of the Ways and Means Committee, which selected Democratic members of other standing committees. He was thus in a position to exercise, at least partially, one important power that had previously belonged to the Speaker. Later, after World War I, the floor leader no longer served as chairman of Ways and Means and his power dwindled.

The Republicans took over Congress in the 1920's, and the House Steering Committee assumed the principal policy-making role. There was still strong sentiment against permitting the Speaker any great degree of policy power. The Republicans had a healthy fear of the specter of Cannonism. This was manifested when Republican members of the House chose Frederick H. Gillett for Speaker over James R. Mann, who had been minority leader since 1911 and was thus a natural candidate for the position. Mann was bypassed because he was considered by some to be an adherent of the old Cannon despotism.

Nevertheless, command gradually accrued again to the speakership. It was not long before Gillett was invited to sit in on the meetings of the decision-making Steering Committee. Later, when Longworth was Speaker, the Steering Committee went into the discard. Major decisions were made by an informal group that included the Speaker, the floor leader, and the party whip. When the Democrats gained control of the House during the last two years of the Hoover Administration, John Nance Garner was elected Speaker and he carried the system of informality even further. Garner had been a member of the House for twenty-eight years and knew all that any man could know about the conduct of its business. Most of the important questions involving party policies were settled by him and a few cronies in afterhours sessions away from the House chamber. He not only was privy to the decisions but was the leader in arriving at them.

Power was coming back to the speakership, even though it was in many respects a different kind of power and in nearly all respects was attained and retained by methods far removed from those used during the rule of Reed and Cannon.

The diffused system of leadership that followed the House Revolution of 1910 had not been without its thoughtful critics. Nobody asked for a return to dictatorship, but complaints were voiced that the new ways fell something short of perfection. For example, Robert Luce, himself a member of Congress, wrote in 1926 (in *Congress: An Explanation*): "The most striking difference between the old and the new methods is that, whereas leadership was then in the open, it is now under cover. Then the Speaker was the recognized center of authority. Now nobody knows who in the last resort decides. . . . It might be said that nowadays the leadership of the House is in commission, with the membership of the commission more or less fluctuating and shadowy."

Another observer, Ch'iu Cha'ng-wei, whose authoritative

The Speaker of the House of Representatives Since 1896 was published in 1928, concluded that, inevitably, "the leadership of the Speaker will pass from its present position to a much stronger one." "How far this tendency will go," he continued, "depends upon two conditions: (1) the character of the person in the Speaker's chair, and (2) the extent of interest the American people show in the House of Representatives." His prediction has been fully realized and in line with the conditions he set.

The power that has been regained by the Speaker is not, of course, absolute. On the other hand, neither is leadership in the House as widely diffused as one might be led to believe by the existence of twenty standing committees—each autonomous, each with its own chairman—plus scores of subcommittees, plus political committees, plus other elective House officials. The Speaker is again the most powerful man in either body of Congress. Although he no longer directly appoints the standing committees, his wishes carry heavy weight in filling vacancies, and he does appoint the select committees. He also names the chairman of the Committee of the Whole, the medium through which the House transacts much of its most important business. In the regular legislative conferences between the President and his party leaders in Congress (when the Executive and Legislative branches are controlled by the same party), the Speaker heads the "Big Four," its other members being the House majority leader, the Vice-President, and the Senate majority leader.

The Speaker has to operate under the rules of the House, to be sure, and those rules bind him rather more tightly now than at times in the past. But, as Sam Rayburn once said (after conceding the necessity of rules in a legislative body), "Leadership can best be exercised through personal friendship and reasonable persuasion." And he added: "If a Speaker is to be successful in his job, his party colleagues in the House have got to want to follow him."

Rayburn spoke from his own knowledge and experience, for

he built the speakership into a position of the greatest influence that had attended it since the days of Cannon, who ran the House under wholly different rules. Rayburn accomplished this, as he said, not by "pounding the desk and giving people hell" but through leading "by persuasion and kindness and the best reason."

This marks an interesting return in concept to the principles regulating the Speaker's duties that were laid down by Henry Clay, the first man to bring strength to the speakership. Clay, on assuming that post for the sixth and last time on December 1, 1823, described those principles as follows:

"They enjoin promptitude and impartiality in deciding the various questions of order as they arise; firmness and dignity in his deportment toward the House; patience, good temper; and courtesy toward the individual members; and the best arrangement and distribution of the talent of the House, in its numerous subdivisions, for the dispatch of the public business; and the fair exhibition of every subject presented for consideration. They especially require of him, in those moments of agitation from which no deliberative assembly is always entirely exempt, to remain cool and unshaken amidst all the storms of debate, carefully guarding the preservation of the permanent laws and rules of the House from being sacrificed to temporary passions, prejudices, or interests."

4

For most—although not for all—Speakers of the House of Representatives, the attainment of the speakership has been the climax of their political careers. Fewer than half the men who have served as Speaker have gone on to seek other offices. Fewer still have actually attained other offices.

Only one Speaker, James K. Polk, became President of the United States. Three others were unsuccessful candidates for President. Henry Clay was three times the Whig candidate and vainly sought the nomination twice more. He was a member of the Senate both before he became Speaker and for a long time after he left the House, and served for four years as Secretary of State. John Bell, who was Speaker for part of the duration of the Twenty-third Congress, was a candidate for President in 1860 on the Constitutional Union ticket. Between his House service and his presidential candidacy, he had served as Secretary of War under President William H. Harrison and as a member of the Senate from 1847 to 1859. And James G. Blaine, Speaker from 1869 to 1875, was the Republican Party's defeated candidate for President in 1884. In addition, after his House service, he was Secretary of State during the presidency of James Garfield and of Benjamin Harrison.

Other Speakers, of course, tried to obtain the presidential nomination of their parties. The one who came closest to succeeding was Champ Clark, who in the famous National Democratic Convention of 1912 was top man in the voting on twenty-nine ballots and actually had a clear majority on eight ballots. In the end, he lost because of the then prevailing rule in the Democratic Convention that the nomination must be made by a two-thirds majority.

Two Speakers, Schuyler Colfax of Indiana and John Nance Garner of Texas, later served as Vice-President. In addition to Clay and Blaine, other Speakers later to become members of the President's Cabinet were Howell Cobb of Georgia, who was Secretary of the Treasury under President Buchanan, and John G. Carlisle of Kentucky, who was President Cleveland's Secretary of the Treasury. Robert M. T. Hunter of Virginia was Secretary of State in the Confederacy.

Cobb also was governor of Georgia just after leaving the House. Other Speakers who served their states as governors were Jonathan Trumbull of Connecticut, Polk, Nathaniel P. Banks of Massachusetts, James L. Orr of South Carolina, and William Pennington of New Jersey.

A number of Speakers other than Clay became members of the Senate. One was Jonathan Dayton of New Jersey, who was Speaker in the Fourth and Fifth Congresses and then went on to the Senate for a six-year term. In 1807, two years after leaving the Senate, he was arrested on charges of treason for conspiring with Aaron Burr, but was never brought to trial. Other Speakers who served in the Senate were Trumbull, Theodore Sedgwick of Massachusetts, Nathaniel Macon of North Carolina, Joseph B. Varnum of Massachusetts, John Bell of Tennessee, Hunter, Robert C. Winthrop of Massachusetts, Blaine, Carlisle, and Frederick H. Gillett, also of Massachusetts.

Other honors came to other Speakers. Philip P. Barbour, a Virginian, became an Associate Justice of the Supreme Court; Langdon Cheves of South Carolina, however, declined such an appointment. Andrew Stevenson, also a Virginian, was Minister to Great Britain from 1836 to 1841, and James L. Orr, another from South Carolina, was Minister to Russia during 1872 and 1873.

In recent years it has become the custom for a Speaker to serve until his death or until his party loses control of the House. Thus John W. McCormack, Democratic floor leader, succeeded to the speakership on the death of Sam Rayburn, and Rayburn had gone from the floor leadership to the speakership when William B. Bankhead died in 1940.

Usually, also, if his party becomes a minority the Speaker steps down to the minority floor leadership, while the former minority leader assumes the post of minority whip, and the deposed whip returns to the status of a rank-and-file member. It is a rather rigid system, although sometimes an incumbent party leader is forced out of his position. At the opening of the Eighty-sixth Congress in January, 1959, for example, the Republican caucus chose Charles A. Halleck of Indiana as minority floor leader to replace Joseph W. Martin, Jr., of Massachusetts, who had been either floor leader or Speaker continuously for twenty years. Such an overthrow of the existing order is exceptional, and the outcome of the secret vote ballot in the caucus was a close seventy-four to seventy. Halleck, at age fifty-eight, had been able to convince his followers that he could provide stronger leadership than Martin, who was seventy-four and had been ill. Also, some Republicans felt that Martin worked too closely with Sam Rayburn and his Democrats.

Long congressional service has come to be a prerequisite for election as Speaker. Up to 1896, the men elected Speaker had served an average of only seven years in the House before their promotion. Since that time, however, the average length of House service of men named to the speakership has been about twenty years. Sam Rayburn was in his twenty-eighth year of service as a Representative when he assumed the Speaker's chair. John W. McCormack had been in the House thirty-three years before he became Speaker.

Along with legislative experience, the Speaker must, above all else, be a man who has gained the confidence, respect, and friendship of a majority—and not just a bare majority—of the members of his party in the House of Representatives. Not possessing these attributes, he could never be elected Speaker. Not retaining them, he could never meet the responsibilities or be able to take advantage of the opportunities of the speakership. It is a most demanding job. For the man born to politics, its rewards can be commensurate with its demands.

II

Star of the West

"THERE IS NO PLACE," observed President James A. Garfield, who formerly had been a member of the House, "where a man finds his own level so certainly and so speedily as in the House of Representatives."

Henry Clay of Kentucky out of Virginia found his level the first day he took his seat, November 4, 1811, for he was immediately elected Speaker of the House of Representatives. No other member of the House, before or since, has been named to the speakership on the first day of his term. Even the Speaker in the First Congress, Frederick A. C. Muhlenberg, was not elected to the post until a month after Congress had convened, for a quorum of the House had not been present until then.

Clay remained in the House, except for two short intervals, until 1825 and was elected Speaker in every Congress of which he was a member—six times in all. Until the durable Sam Rayburn came along in the following century, Clay held the record for length of service as Speaker. His tenure of service is of far less significance, however, than the lasting effect he had on the House. From the first, he set out deliberately and boldly to use the speakership to advance his own political goals and the goals of those men who stood with him. This had not been done before.

Six men had preceded Clay as Speaker of the House. None of the six, able and honorable men though they were, made an enduring imprint on the "popular body" of the American Congress. Indeed, they would hardly have considered it fitting that they try to do so. The Speaker was regarded as the moderator of the House. The early Speakers performed the duties of their office by keeping order, or by trying to, by putting questions to a vote, and by signing bills and other documents. They did not hold that they were there to run things.

No such passive role would have been possible for Henry Clay. He was different from his predecessors. They had been, literally, Fathers of the American Revolution. Clay was a Son of the Revolution. They had come from the Thirteen Original States. Clay, although born in Virginia, had from young manhood been a citizen of the new western state of Kentucky, and his temperament and his ideas alike were colored by the frontier excitement of change and growth. The earlier Speakers, if experienced in the holding of public office, could hardly be called politicians in the modern sense of the word. Clay was, simply and almost exclusively, a political being. Thirty-four years of age when he became Speaker, he already had back of him a dozen years of active involvement in politics.

1

Henry Clay was born in Hanover County, Virginia, April 12, 1777. His father, a Baptist minister, died when Clay was a child of four. His early education was sparse and he added but little to it in later years, justifying John Quincy Adams' judgment that Clay was "only half educated." But Clay, though he was not a scholar, had an eager and inquiring mind and was quick to grasp and retain from available books what was useful to him. He studied law under George Wythe, the first professor of law in America and a teacher of Washington and Jefferson, and was admitted to the bar at Richmond in 1797.

The twenty-year-old lawyer liked to talk and he talked well, his face growing animated and his blue-gray eyes flashing when he warmed to an argument. His world was filled with new and challenging ideas, which he met with bold confidence. In particular, young Clay and his Richmond companions were devotees of the French Revolution. They addressed one another as "Citizen," avidly copied French fashions, and even at times dated their letters from the birth of the French Revolution. For them, and for many other Americans, the events in France had marked the beginning of a brave new world.

Even as a young man, Clay was supremely sure of himself. Bernard Mayo has pointed out that "he was never in the slightest degree, even in his early youth, awed by the presence of anyone." He took his self-confidence with him when he moved to Lexington, Kentucky, not long after his admission to the bar. Kentucky was then populated largely by former Virginians, who impressed Clay with their public-spirited pride in their new home. He noted that the Kentuckians "eagerly recommend to strangers the country they inhabit as the best part of the United States, . . . where all the inhabitants were brought together through the love of liberty and independence."

Clay's own metamorphosis from a scion of the Old Dominion to a son of the New West proceeded rapidly. With his extroverted nature, his convivial temperament, and his lack of timidity, he was remarkably successful from the first in both his personal relations and his professional practice. He turned his adroit tongue and resourceful mind to good use in the often tumultuous "court days" in Lexington. His forthright approach to issues involved in his legal cases was completely in tune with the spirit of the frontier, and he quickly built a reputation as a lawyer who won cases. He prospered in his new home, married Lucretia Hart, cousin of a future senator from Missouri, Thomas Hart Benton, and started to raise a family.

The young attorney soon found himself enthralled more by politics than by the practice of law. When he was only twenty-two he served as a member of a state constitutional convention that had been called to inject more democracy into the state government and to make possible the gradual emancipation of slaves in Kentucky. Clay's speeches attacking autocratic control of the government attracted enthusiastic attention. Once he was carried triumphantly from the speaker's stand by a Lexington audience, surely a heady experience for a youngster of twenty-two.

Clay was elected to the Kentucky legislature in 1803. When he was twenty-nine, a few months short of the age limit set in the Federal Constitution, he was elected to an unexpired term in the United States Senate when John Adair resigned his seat. He went back to Kentucky to serve again in the state legislature in 1808–09 and was chosen Speaker of the lower house. A year later he was elected to another unexpired term in the Senate following the resignation of Buckner Thruston, but he was not happy there, agreeing perhaps with Washington Irving's acid estimate of the Senators as "national greybeards" who "hold all wit and humor in abomination." The livelier House of Representatives beckoned enticingly to the young man from Kentucky. He campaigned for and won the House seat from the Lexington district, and was off with vigor and confidence to a new career.

Throughout his long political life Clay was given nicknames by friends and foes that revealed much about the man. In the end, he had more nicknames than any other public figure of his time. He was known variously as "The Cock of Kentucky," "The Kentucky Hotspur," "The War Hawk," and, more prosaically, "The Great Kentuckian." Banquet toastmasters introduced him floridly as "Harry of the West" and "Prince Hal." "Judas of the West" was one of the printable appellations bestowed upon him by the opposition. He was called "The Compromiser" and, as his talents in the area of bringing opposing forces together came increasingly into play and were widely recognized, "The Great Compromiser" and "The Great Pacificator." He was labeled "The Great Commoner" long before William Jennings Bryan was born. In his later days he was "The Old Prince" to those who honored him.

Clay earned some of these nicknames. Others were hung upon him like garlands because, in an emotional age, he was a man who aroused deep-seated emotions in other men. In either case, almost every phase of his career is marked with a nickname.

He himself was highly emotional. He loved and was loved by many, yet he was capable, in a moment of angry disappointment, of railing that his friends were "not worth the powder and shot it would take to kill them." In a time when oratory was highly esteemed, he could weave with his tongue a magic spell over the minds of men, but John Quincy Adams, who had the Adams habit of writing down everything, noted in his journal that Clay "is so ardent, dogmatical, and overbearing that it is extremely difficult to preserve the temper of friendly society with him." Adams admitted that he and the Kentuckian were somewhat alike in this respect.

Nor was it only in his emotional reactions that Clay was inconsistent. Once in Congress a long-winded gentleman from Virginia chided him, "You, sir, speak for the present generation, but I speak for posterity," and Clay shot back, "Yes, and you seem resolved to speak until the arrival of your audience." But he himself could hold the floor of the House of Representatives for two full days with a single speech.

Clay said of himself, "Rocked in the cradle of the Revolution, I was born a democrat." He kept most of his democratic convictions through most of his life, but by temperament he was an aristocrat and in practice he was often an autocrat. After Clay's death a friend remarked of him that never in his life had the Old Prince felt that he was in the presence of a man superior to himself. And, when he chose to, he could make that conviction known.

He was impractical enough to lose eight thousand dollars in a single evening's session of "brag," the early American equivalent of poker. (A friend once said to Mrs. Clay, "Isn't it a pity your husband gambles so much?" "Oh, I don't know," that lady replied calmly, "Mr. Clay usually wins.") But he was sufficiently practical to ask, when a Quaker visitor to his Kentucky plantation implored him to free his slaves, whether the Friends were prepared to pay him the fifteen thousand dollars he reckoned the slaves were worth on the market.

Clay was all his life a charmer of both men and women. The warmth of his nature demanded human companionship, and his ego demanded love and admiration from those around him. He used his friends, of course, to his own ends, extracting both entertainment and information from them. Few evinced resentment at being used. In the opinion of the American historian James Ford Rhodes, "No man has been loved as the people of the United States loved Henry Clay." Yet neither his personal popularity nor his political genius brought him the presidential prize he assiduously sought for a quarter of a century.

He was direct and candid in his relations with others. Still, his native charm aroused distrust in some and his genius for compromise caused him at times to be charged with duplicity. He prided himself on being close to the people. But he was no hail fellow well met, and when he walked the streets of Lexington no man ever clapped him on the back and called him "Hal" or "Harry."

Despite his brilliant mind, he was neither profound nor given to thinking in abstract terms. His easy success as a lawyer was based less on a deep knowledge of law than on his empathy with other men and a swift understanding of how best to win them to his way of thinking. In an important legal case, Clay felt certain that he had eleven of the jurors on his side, but the face of the twelfth, a stubborn-looking man from the Kentucky hill country, showed no sympathy. Halting suddenly in the middle of an eloquent peroration, Clay leveled a finger at this juryman and said, "My friend, a pinch of snuff, if you please."

Taken aback at this personal attention, the hillman blurted out, "I don't snuff, Mr. Clay, but I chaws." Clay won the case.

He was a man whose nature contained supreme self-contradictions. Finally, that mattered less than the fact that, in the words of George Bancroft, "neither in public nor in private did Henry Clay know how to be dull."

2

The Eleventh Congress suffered heavy casualties at the hands of the voters on election day. Seventy of the 142 members of the House of Representatives in the Twelfth Congress, which assembled in Washington for a special session in November, 1811, were freshmen. Many of the older members long in control of the House were among those not re-elected. Those who did come back found a changed situation. Power now was centered in new, young members from the West and the lower South—men from the new states or from the frontier regions of the Original Thirteen.

Their youth was particularly striking. Clay and all those who were to work most closely with him in the House had been born after the signing of the Declaration of Independence. Clay himself, at thirty-four, actually was one of the oldest. John C. Calhoun and William Lowndes of South Carolina were each twenty-nine. Richard M. Johnson, Clay's Kentucky colleague, was thirty. John Adams Harper of New Hampshire was thirty-one, and Langdon Cheves of South Carolina was only a year older. Felix Grundy, Tennessee, was the same age as Clay. These members were the stalwarts of the Clay forces in the House.

Most of them and most of the other young members—in fact, two-thirds of the total House membership—were lawyers. Many of them, in contrast to the new Speaker with his scant formal learning, had received the best education to be had in the country at that time. They had a vision, put into words for them by Henry Clay, of a *new* United States, a truly independent nation. This was not merely a different Congress from the Eleventh; it was a different kind of Congress. This new House of Representatives was prepared to exert national leadership. And it had a different kind of Speaker. "If he is like anybody," a contemporary said of Clay, "he does not know it. He has never studied models, and if he had, his pride would have rescued him from the fault of imitation."

Clay was in tune with the West, and the people of the West were fired with resentment against Great Britain. The Westerners were convinced that England was back of the Indian uprisings against the Americans. Further, their nationalistic sentiments were outraged by Britain's violations of the rights of neutrals in the war between England and France and by the impressment of American seamen into the British Navy.

As early as January, 1806, Clay had written to Attorney General John Breckinridge that war with Great Britain would be popular in the West. "Perhaps this is a fortunate moment to repress European aggression," he suggested, "and to evince to the world that Americans appreciate their rights in such a way as will induce them, when violated, to engage in war with alacrity and effect." In speeches during his campaign for the House seat, he strongly supported the movement to bring about a declaration of war against Great Britain. Clay felt that the national honor demanded war. He was as sensitive to matters that affected the national honor as he was to matters affecting his personal honor—and sensitivity regarding the latter led to his participation in three duels in his lifetime.

Even before Congress formally convened, Clay had become the chosen leader of the youthful "War Hawks" in their own pre-session caucuses. In the formal party caucus before the session opened, he received seventy-five votes, while the antiwar candidate, William Bibb of Georgia, got only thirty-eight and Nathaniel Macon, Speaker in the Seventh, Eighth and Ninth Congresses, a paltry three. His adherents went on to sweep him into the speakership on the first day of the session. Their Republican party had an overwhelming majority in the House, 105 to 37 Federalists.

This majority, however, was by no means completely united. Some of the moderates feared the impetuous, impatient War Hawks. New Englanders in general—with notable exceptions such as New Hampshire's Harper—and some Southern members were strongly opposed to the nationalistic war aims of Clay and his followers. Old John Randolph of Virginia, born to make trouble and seeing power slipping from his hands, was among those who were openly scornful of the "horde of upstart patriots" and particularly of their leader, who, Randolph bitterly sneered, "strided from the floor of the Hall as soon as he entered it to the Speaker's chair."

The Federalists in the House, although reduced in number, were able and experienced men. They had a thoroughly seasoned leader in Josiah Quincy of Boston.

In the White House, President Madison vacillated.

Clay was sharply aware of all these factors. He knew, too, that cautious eyes, even skeptical eyes, were watching to see if he would be able to control the House. Neither of the last two Speakers had been capable of coping with Quincy's skilled obstructionism or of preventing Randolph from riding roughshod over the rights of other members. Realistic knowledge of what he faced did not make the Kentuckian fearful. Before his election he had said he preferred "the turbulent House" over the Senate. The turbulence itself was no doubt one of the reasons for his preference.

In his speech of acceptance, the new Speaker declared his purpose would be to facilitate the transaction of business "in the most agreeable manner." He did not say that he held the Speaker's duties and responsibilities to go far beyond anything contemplated in the past. But the way he proceeded with the first business of organizing the House spoke plainly. He proved himself no less a genius as an organizer than as an orator.

It had become clear that the President was looking to Congress to set the policy of his Administration. He sent a message urging its members to put the nation "in an armor and an attitude demanded by the crisis." If not a summons to war, this at least went beyond anything Madison had been willing to say in the past. It seemed to Clay the right beginning. He organized the House in accordance with his own interpretation of the spirit of the President's message. He named War Hawks as chairman of the all-important committees on Foreign Relations, Military Affairs, and Ways and Means. He made sure also that each committee had a majority of members who thought as he did about the necessity of going to war with England.

Considerable uproar followed the announcement of the committees. The old-guard Republicans were resentful at having their accustomed power drastically curtailed. Randolph sought to uphold his reputation for browbeating House Speakers as well as the general membership by taking the floor for a falsetto-voiced denunciation of "the boy dictator." The Federalists, rising in partisan wrath, cried that Clay had assumed "monstrous" power.

The new Speaker permitted everyone to have his say, but the committee appointments stood.

So did the rulings he promptly began to hand down to keep the House in order. In the past the House had been stigmatized as a notorious cockpit of disorder. The "Cock of Kentucky" was the man to take command of a cockpit.

It took some doing. Members had a habit of drowning out a colleague they did not want to hear by sheer volume of noise. They talked among themselves in loud tones, went into coughing fits, banged their desk covers, and used every other possible means of discouraging debate on measures of which they disapproved. The rules placed no limit on debate. The filibuster flourished in the House to a greater extent than it ever has in the Senate, members frequently halting the disposition of business for hours at a time with rambling speeches on virtually any topic except the one under consideration.

Clay used a combination of charm, logic, and forcefulness to bring some measure of order to the proceedings. Even the primitive rules that existed had not been strictly enforced by past Speakers, but they were enforced by Clay. Later, under his guidance, the House approved and then strengthened the motion of the "previous question" as a means of cutting off debate and bringing up for an immediate vote the main question then before the House. The rule, Clay said, was "nothing more than a declaration of the House that it had heard enough and would proceed to decide."

The Speaker's tact and geniality enabled him to tighten the reins without giving offense to the general membership of the House. He also sought to restore the sadly missing element of personal dignity to the body. Thus a member who persisted in being out of order was firmly instructed by the Speaker to take his seat. A member who went to sleep at his desk received a tart message from the Chair that he should either stay awake or go home and that, staying, he should remove his feet from the table. Old Randolph, who liked to bring his hunting dogs into the House chamber, tried that once with Clay, who immediately ordered the doorkeeper to remove the dogs. "In the past," admiringly reported Clay's friend, Harper, "no one dared turn the dogs out."

In the face of the Speaker's firmness, the uproar over his committee appointments died away. The Federalists themselves came to admit that the appointments were "judicious." And a Federalist writer for the Philadelphia *Gazette*, reporting on the Speaker's victory, said it was to be regretted that his position would prevent him from displaying his genius for debate.

He was mistaken in his man, of course, as Clay soon demonstrated by taking the floor for a two-hour speech on behalf of a bill calling for a substantial addition to the Regular Army. There was no law or rule against the Speaker engaging in debate, but it was something that had rarely been done. Clay did it often. He was not deterred by such criticism as Quincy's sour characterization of him during the war debates as "a statesman with pinfeathers not yet grown."

That may be put down as a partisan estimate, for Clay was powerful in debate. Always one to be attracted by contests, he never neglected his homework in preparing for a major speech. He invariably had the facts. "He never spoke," said Lincoln, in later years, "merely to be heard." He did not indulge—at least not in the House, although speeches at political gatherings were a different matter—in the thunderous emptiness that was fashionable in the oratory of the day, but he used the marvelous

31

organ of his voice with perfect control and great effectiveness. Although he was not a conventionally handsome man—his nose was too large, his mouth too wide—the imposing bearing of his six-foot frame and the expressiveness of his face combined to give him a distinguished appearance, the appearance of a statesman. The genius he had shown as a young lawyer in Kentucky for knowing just what note would most appeal to his listeners was an additional factor in his ability more often than not to carry the day when he was determined to do so.

The Kentuckian had never been more determined about anything than he was about war with England. To those who asked what could be gained by war, he flung back the reply, "What are we not to lose by peace? Commerce—character—a nation's best treasure, honor!" He and his War Hawks went steadily ahead with preparations for war. Even when their majority became restive and uncertain, Clay and his stalwarts persisted to drive through, to cajole through, and to compromise through the legislative acts for defense and the appropriations needed to pay—or to borrow—for defense.

When Madison sent to Congress a resolution declaring war the Federalists embarked on a gigantic filibuster to compensate for their lack of numerical strength. They organized their members into relay teams, one member picking up from another in order to keep control of the House floor in their hands. Under the rules there was no way to stop the filibuster, so the War Hawks found themselves forced to resort to the same disorderly tactics their leader had been working to suppress. Late one night a group of them burst noisily into the House chamber in the middle of a long-drawn-out speech by a Federalist member. Shouting and laughing, they proceeded to pick up the spittoons with which the House was equipped and to toss them around the chamber. Frightened, dismayed, the speaker holding the floor gave up and took his seat. One of the War Hawks immediately moved the previous question, in accordance with the rule Clay had influenced the House to approve. The motion was adopted, effectively bringing the filibuster to an end, and the Speaker himself then put the main question. That was approved, too, by a vote of seventy-nine to forty-nine.

After a few days of argument by the more reluctant Senate, that body also approved the declaration of war. On June 18, 1812, President Madison signed the act, and a state of war existed between the United States and Great Britain.

The triumphant first-term Speaker of the House, Quincy declared, "was the man whose influence and power more than any other produced the War of 1812." It was "Mr. Clay's war."

It *was* Mr. Clay's war, and from beginning to end he led the way in all legislative activity pertaining to it. He did everything but fight in the war, and even at that there was one wild and absurd moment when Madison seriously considered making Clay the Commander-in-chief of the American forces. The moment passed—fortunately, since, for all his governmental genius, Clay had no knowledge of military strategy—but almost everything else that could have gone wrong with the progress of the war did go wrong.

In his excellent study, *The True Henry Clay,* Joseph M. Rogers stated the facts plainly:

"Clay had now declared war against the greatest naval power in the world and one of the strongest in the field. . . . To meet this foe, the War Hawks gave the President a loan which he could not float, taxes that he could not collect, a Regular Army he could not raise, militia he could not use, and permitted him to retain the remnant of the Navy founded by John Adams and everlastingly reprobated by every anti-Federalist. . . . To Clay's credit be it said that he was the Navy's most ardent champion. His eloquence could force a declaration of war, but it could not wring money from the people's pockets nor incite them to energetic endeavor."

But Clay could try even that. When the session of Congress ended, he turned his energies to a one-man recruiting campaign and journeyed over the country to encourage young men to join the Army. He met with much success, but the Army did not—it suffered one defeat after another. The untrained American militia was led across the border to Canada by way of Detroit, but was soon withdrawn; then the British struck back by taking Detroit. The garrison at Fort Dearborn, the present site of Chicago, was evacuated. An American attempt to capture Niagara failed. So did an assault against Montreal when General Henry Dearborn was unable to get his troops to cross the Canadian border because they had not signed up to fight outside the United States.

By the time Congress reconvened, many members were for giving up the war and seeking the most advantageous peace that could be had. Clay berated them for their timidity and, again stepping down from the Speaker's chair for a series of addresses on the House floor, urgently demanded that the conflict be pressed with vigor and determination.

During one such address by the Speaker, his constant adversary, John Randolph, interrupted to pose a sarcastic query: "After you have raised these 25,000 men, shall we form a committee of public safety to carry on the war, or shall we depute the power to the Speaker? Shall we declare that, the Executive not being capable of discerning the public interest or not having spirit to pursue it, we have appointed a committee to take the President and Cabinet into custody?"

But Clay won his point. The war continued. It was still, or again, Mr. Clay's war.

Madison, however, was eager to bring hostilities to an end. He wanted to accept the offer of the Czar of Russia to act as a mediator between the United States and Britain. The British rejected this proposal but did agree to enter into direct negotiations with the United States. Clay resigned the speakership to accept appointment as one of five members of the American Commission to negotiate a peace treaty. John Quincy Adams was head of the Commission, and he and Clay were from the first in conflict not only over the terms of the treaty but also about their entire approach to the task at hand. Other members of the Commission were Albert Gallatin, James A. Bayard, and Jonathan Russell.

The American group arrived in Ghent late in June, 1814, but had to wait for more than a month before the British representatives arrived. Negotiations began then and continued until near the end of the year. The Americans had a difficult time. They were placed at a serious disadvantage when the defeat of Napoleon's army defending Paris made it possible for the British to turn more seriously to the conflict with their former colonies.

The British commissioners repeatedly suggested terms of peace that the Americans, and Clay in particular, considered wholly untenable, even insolent. For example, the British started by proposing that a great section of the Middle West be set aside as neutral Indian country and that Great Britain should take most of northern New York and New England and all of the south bank of the St. Lawrence River and the Niagara. The Americans were asked to agree that their country would build no forts on the lakes and would keep no navy there. Also, they were to give up their rights to the inshore fisheries.

Clay stormed that the British commissioners acted as if they were dealing with a defeated enemy. He clashed frequently with Adams and with other members of the Commission, some of whom he felt were altogether too eager for peace at any price and too ready to accede to terms that he considered disgraceful. Adams, busily scribbling in his diary in the early dawn (about the time that Clay and his convivial companions would roll in from a night spent with whiskey and cards), noted disapprovingly that the Kentuckian was "for playing brag with the British plenipotentiaries."

"He asked me," Adams confided to his journal, "if I knew how to play brag. I had forgotten how. He said the art of it was to beat your adversary by holding your hand, with a solemn and confident phiz, and outbragging him. He asked Mr. Bayard if it was not. 'Ay,' said Mr. Bayard, 'but you may lose the game by bragging until the adversary sees the weakness of your hand.' And Mr. Bayard added to me, 'Mr. Clay is for bragging a million against a cent.' "

Sometimes Clay won at brag and sometimes he lost, but this time it was a team game and he was not permitted to call every play. In the end, all important issues were compromised or action on them was deferred. On Christmas Eve, Clay joined the other commissioners in signing the treaty, but he did so with the utmost reluctance, growling that they had "made a damned bad treaty."

He stayed on in Europe with Adams and Albert Gallatin to negotiate a commercial agreement with Great Britain, given heart for the task by the news of Jackson's victory at New Orleans. On his return to the United States in September, 1815, he found that the peace to which he had so grudgingly agreed was popular with the folks at home. His own standing in Kentucky was higher than ever, a fact for which Joseph Rogers' book gives this at least partial explanation: "From time to time the government published dispatches in which Clay's demands on certain positions as a *sine qua non* were frequent. This mystified the unlettered Kentuckians until one of them suddenly discovered that *Sine, Qua,* and *Non* were three islands in the Passamaquoddy Bay. 'And Hennery Clay will never give them up, if we fight forever.'"

The War of 1812 went a long way toward transforming the former colonies into a nation. When Mrs. Frances Trollope came to the United States in 1827 to gather material for her scathing book on the domestic manners of the Americans, she found her hosts were happy about the war and the way it had turned out. Their manner of expressing this, that redoubtable lady reported, was usually "in a manner more comic than offensive." People would talk to her, she said, in this fashion: "Well, now, I think your government must just be fit to hang themselves for that last war they cooked up; it has been the ruin of you, I expect, for it has just been the making of us."

The loyal voters in Clay's home district clearly felt that he had done well by them. They had re-elected him to the House of Representatives while he was absent in Europe, and on the first day of the new session he was again chosen Speaker of the House.

Henry Clay was not a man who enjoyed being made to appear a fool. As a lawyer, he was once approached by a prominent citizen who had been accused by a neighbor of stealing a "bee gum," the colloquial Kentucky name for a beehive. This was somewhat equivalent to being accused of horse stealing in the cow country, so the prominent citizen was understandably disturbed.

Clay accepted the case and told the man to meet him at the courthouse with his witnesses. The client appeared, but he brought no witnesses. A strong case was made against him by witnesses for the accuser. Clay did his best by delivering an eloquent speech regarding his client's good standing and reputation for integrity. But it was not enough. The jury took only a few moments to return with a verdict of guilty.

As the irate lawyer strode from the room, the prominent citizen grabbed him by his coattails, crying, "Mr. Clay! Mr. Clay! We've lost our case."

Clay turned a cold look on him and bellowed, "Yes, we've lost our case, but, by God, we've got our bee gum!"

Possession of the bee gum, figuratively speaking, was of increasing importance to Clay after his return from Ghent. His protracted stay in Europe had the effect of sharpening still further his enthusiasm for everything American. Advancing the material well-being of the nation in general and of the West in particular became his prime concern. It was during the decade following the end of the war with Great Britain that he developed his "American System," a program that grew out of his spirit of optimistic nationalism.

The three most important features of the American System called for extending federal financial assistance in the construction of internal improvements such as roads and canals, for the establishment of a national bank, and for erecting a protective tariff umbrella over American industry. Later the program was enlarged to include distribution to the states, according to their population, of surplus funds from public land sales.

Claw saw a tremendous era of expansion ahead for the United States now that, as he felt, the threat of aggression from the former mother country had been removed.

These ideas split the Republicans. The division was hastened by the fact that after the war the Federalists were virtually out of business as a political party. The Republicans, lacking opposition from outside their ranks, proceeded to provide their own opposition. The old group, the advocates of states' rights, stood pat on a strict interpretation of the limiting powers of the Constitution. The new National Republicans called for a liberal interpretation of the Constitution to give the federal government greater latitude in meeting the problems of national growth.

Clay, naturally, was with the new Republicans. He and John C. Calhoun, who held nationalistic sentiments paralleling Clay's, became the foremost congressional champions of the new party's policies. The Speaker refused proffered appointments as minister to Russia and to England, declaring that his place was in Congress pushing his legislative program. He favored planned development of the country and he wanted the process to be financed with federal money. He had no patience with those who held that expenditures for building roads and digging waterways would contravene the Constitution. He made the startling prediction that at some future time the United States would have a population of a hundred million. When that time came, he said, national aid for internal improvements would be recognized as essential and would be held constitutional. Why wait? he wanted to know.

He brought about the passage in 1817 of a bill setting up a permanent fund for such improvements. But the measure was vetoed by Madison the day before he went out of office and denounced as unconstitutional by Monroe in his first message to Congress. Clay was, of course, in this matter ahead of the two Presidents and of most of his party and of his times. The principles on which he based his argument for constitutionality of the bill for internal improvements long ago came to be taken for granted by the great majority of Americans.

The Speaker enjoyed better fortune with another feature of his American System, the establishment of a national bank. Before the war he had opposed the national bank, but now he spoke out strongly on behalf of a report to Congress by Calhoun that recommended the immediate chartering of such an institution. There was an economic depression in the country, the currency was in a condition of chaos, and a federally chartered bank would be safe from the threat of foreign control. So Clay argued, and he and Calhoun prevailed.

While the Kentuckian had sound and high-minded reasons for favoring the establishment of the bank, once it was a reality he had no aversion to obtaining political and personal benefits from its existence. He used the vast influence given him by his powerful position in the House to get branches of the bank established at Lexington and Louisville in his home state. He suggested that several of his prominent Kentucky friends be named directors of these branches, and tried to rent to the bank a building that he owned in Lexington. Also, he became an attorney for the bank at a comfortable annual retainer fee and was active in prosecuting defaulting debtors in Kentucky and Ohio.

Clay favored protective tariffs for essentially the same reason that he favored internal improvements. Both, he maintained, were necessary for proper development of the growing country. The products of the inland West—including the considerable amounts of Kentucky cordage produced by his wife's family—could compete in the markets of the East only if adequate transportation facilities were available and protection was given against foreign producers. As he further developed his program, he placed more emphasis on independence for American industry than on safeguards for American products and wages.

"The truth is," he declared, "and it is vain to disguise it, that we are a sort of independent colony of England—politically free, commercially slaves."

He was largely responsible for the tariff law of 1816, enacted over the opposition of Daniel Webster and other New Englanders. Four years later he drove a more stringent bill through the House, but it was lost in the Senate.

In arguing for the 1820 bill, Clay expressed an opinion about child labor that might well have caused him to be drubbed out of public life if he had been speaking a century or so later. He told the House that on a recent visit to New England he had been gratified to find so many young boys and girls working in industrial plants. Too many people in the country were idle, he said, and added: "Can it be doubted that if the crowds of little mendicant boys and girls who infest this edifice, and assail us at its very thresholds, as we come in and go out, begging for a cent, were employed in some manufacturing establishment, it would be better for them and the city?"

Clay was out of Congress for two years—he needed money and turned his attention to his law practice—and when he came back he again took up the tariff fight. Now he saw the "sole object" of the protective tariff as being "to tax the produce of foreign industry with the view of promoting American industry." Hard times had continued, so this was a potent argument.

Clay made a two-day speech in the House on March 30–31, 1824, setting forth in full his arguments for increasing the protective tariff. Clement Eaton has written, in *Henry Clay and the Art of American Politics,* that "the speech was one of the best cases for a protective tariff ever made in the United States, and became the classic argument for the policy of protection." The Speaker did not depend solely on his own persuasion, but had his lieutenants out soliciting votes on the floor and in the cloakrooms. When the vote came on April 16, several Representatives who had been absent because of illness were carried into the House chamber so that their votes could be recorded. The bill was passed with a majority of only five votes, 107 to 102, and subsequently went through the Senate and became law.

The Kentucky Representative could be opportunistic as well as patriotic, sectional as well as broadly nationalistic. His American System revealed all these qualities. He had been bitten by the presidential bug following his return from Europe in 1815 and many of his actions afterwards showed that he had been bitten hard. He had both personal and local political reasons for his advocacy of a protective tariff and federal aid for internal improvements. He and his in-laws were producers of hemp. Kentucky hemp could not meet foreign competition without tariff protection. And how could such products of the West get to Eastern markets without adequate, federally financed transportation facilities? Again, the tariff act of 1824 placed a heavy duty on bagging cloth for cotton bales— and this cloth was a principal product of factories in the Lexington congressional district.

Yet there was more to Clay's fight for his American System than economic or political self-interest. His motives might have been mixed—Jefferson in 1818 charged him with "rallying an opposition to the Administration" because of personal ambition—but in the main he was moved by his conviction that the United States ought to be commercially as well as politically independent of the Old World. Significantly, he had a vision of the common cause of the United States and Latin America. His powerful voice was raised in the House of Representatives to offer encouragement to men who were fighting in the second decade of the nineteenth century for South American liberation. At the same time he warned against a paternalistic attitude on the part of the United States.

"Anxious as I am," he told the House in May of 1818, "that they should have free government, we have no right to prescribe for them. They are, and ought to be, the sole judges for themselves. But I am strongly inclined to believe that they will in most if not in all parts of their country establish free government. . . . They will establish their independence, and secure the enjoyment of those rights and blessings which rightfully belong to them."

This encouragement to Latin American countries at the beginning of their struggle for independence and the wise counsel regarding the policy of the United States reflected no narrow viewpoint.

John Quincy Adams, in a diary entry dated March 9, 1821, summed up his feelings about his ofttime antagonist and frequent ally. "Clay is an eloquent man, with very popular manners and great political management," Adams noted. "He is, like almost all the eminent men of this country, only half educated. His school has been the world, and in that he is proficient. His morals, public and private, are loose, but he has all the virtues indispensable to a popular man. As he is the very first distinguished man the Western country has presented as a statesman to the Union, they are proportionally proud of him, and being a native of Virginia, he has all the benefits of that clannish preference which Virginia has always given her sons. . . . Clay's temper is impetuous, and his ambition impatient. . . . Clay has large and liberal views of public affairs, and that sort of generosity which attaches individuals to his person. As President of the Union, his Administration would be a perpetual succession of intrigue and management within the Legislature. It would also be sectional in its spirit, and sacrifice all other interests to that of the Western country and the slave-holders. But his principles relative to internal improvements would produce results honorable and useful to the nation."

Four years after writing this, Adams, as President, appointed Clay to succeed him as Secretary of State.

4

"Of all men upon earth," said Clay in a moment of introspection, "I am the least attached to the productions of my own mind. No man upon earth is more ready than I am to surrender everything which I have proposed and to accept in lieu of it anything which is better."

This miniature self-portrait of the Kentucky Speaker has not been hailed as completely true to life. Perhaps closer to the truth is Adams' characterization of Clay as "rancorously benevolent." Clay wanted to do right, perhaps even would "rather be right than President." But he also wanted other men to do right, and if their ideas of right differed from his he spoke eloquently of the difference, and his views did not suffer from the comparison he made.

Yet he was, in truth, the Great Compromiser.

Basically, his spirit of compromise was born out of his intense humanness, for he was not a weak man and no one would have accused him of lacking the courage of his convictions. He simply was possessed of an understanding that made it possible for him not merely to grasp the viewpoint of another but also in some cases actually to adopt that viewpoint, sometimes with modifications, as his own. He felt that if one did not at the outset take too intransigent a stand, an accommodation was always in the realm of possibility. If one did not state one's own opinion in too unyielding a manner, one might always by giving a little here gain a great deal there.

In a somewhat more realistic statement than that in which he declared his lack of attachment to what his own mind had produced, Clay said: "I go for honorable compromise wherever it can be made. Life itself is but a compromise between death and life, the struggle continuing throughout our whole existence, until the great destroyer finally triumphs. All legislation, all government, all society is founded upon the principle of mutual concession, politeness, comity, courtesy; upon these everything is based. . . . Let him who elevates himself above humanity, above its weaknesses, its infirmities, its wants, its necessities, say, if he pleases, I never will compromise, but let no one who is not above the frailties of our common nature disdain compromise."

The most famous of his accomplishments in this field was the Missouri Compromise of 1821. The proposed constitution for Missouri carried a provision prohibiting the entrance of free Negroes into the state. This provision brought violent protests from antislavery congressmen, endangering the admission of Missouri to the Union. Clay was able to bring about the appointment of a joint committee of the House and the Senate, which favorably reported a compromise the Kentuckian had previously presented. Under this middle-ground solution the Missouri legislature was to agree that the state's constitution would never be interpreted so as to take away from citizens of other states who entered Missouri the rights and privileges guaranteed them by the United States Constitution. The House of Representatives passed this compromise by the narrow margin of six votes, eighty-seven to eighty-one, an almost singlehanded accomplishment by Clay. The Senate also approved the measure, and on the condition worked out by Clay the state of Missouri was admitted to the Union on August 10, 1821.

Even in his first months as Speaker, when he was pushing for war with England with all the strength he had gathered to the position, Clay was considerate of those who opposed him. Although he made certain that his adherents were in the majority on the committees he named, he did not ignore the minority. He was even accused by extreme partisans, then and many times thereafter, of being too liberal to the opposition.

Nor did he regard his ability to compromise as an inclination to be weak. His rulings as Speaker were firm and unassailable. Many years later, counseling a newly elected Speaker, Robert C. Winthrop, Clay told him: "Decide, decide promptly, and never give your reasons for the decision. The House will sustain your decision, but there will always be men to cavil and quarrel about your reasons."

That was Clay's basic policy. He made the decisions and they stood. Yet he could say, and mean, "It is a rule with me, when acting either in a public or a private character, to attempt nothing more than what there exists a prospect of accomplishment." He learned that politics is the art of the possible long before it became trite to say so. And when he played

the game by ear, relying on his intuition, he was a master prac-
titioner of that art.

If he abandoned intuition and tried to reason out political
matters on the basis of logic, he sometimes went astray. For
example, he no doubt considered it logical enough that in 1816
he should support a bill increasing the salary of members of
Congress from six dollars a day (twelve dollars for the Speaker
of the House)—for days that Congress was in session—to fifteen
hundred dollars a year. That amounted to an increase of only
about six hundred dollars annually. However, Clay's support
of the measure caused him the only trouble he ever had in
being re-elected the Representative from the Lexington district. The law applied to the session of the Fourteenth Congress that passed it and thus was popularly—or, rather, not at
all popularly—known as the "back pay" bill. The retroactive
feature particularly enraged the voters. In the following election, some of the ablest men in Congress lost their seats. Clay
himself had to engage in the kind of intensive personal cam-
paigning he had not found necessary since the first time he ran
for the House.

This was the campaign during which an old hunter in Kentucky told Clay that, although he had always supported him
before, he would not support him this time because of the back-
pay law. The candidate, promptly meeting the voter on his
own ground, asked if the hunter owned a good rifle.

"Yes."

"Did it ever flash [without firing]?" Clay inquired.

"Yes. But only once."

"And what did you do with the rifle when it flashed? Throw
it away?"

"No. I picked the flint and tried it again."

"Have I ever flashed except on this bill?"

"No."

"Well," Clay demanded, "will you throw me away?"

"No, Mr. Clay," returned the hunter. "I will try you again."

Enough voters tried him again to enable Clay to go back

45

to Washington. He reported wonderingly to other members that never in his career had he seen such universal opposition among the people to any legislative measure. Many old friends in the House were gone because of the back-pay bill. All the members from Ohio, Delaware, and Vermont, and most of those from Georgia, Maryland, and South Carolina, were defeated. The pay increase was promptly repealed and new legislation was passed setting congressional salaries at eight dollars a day.

Sometimes the Great Compromiser would not yield an inch, and the refusal did not always place him in an appealing light. He had felt rather confident that Monroe would name him Secretary of State, a position he wanted desperately because he regarded it as a stepping-stone to the presidency. When Adams was named instead, he sulked. He would not attend the inaugural ceremony, and though he may not have been wholly responsible, the use of the House chamber was refused for the ceremony. Monroe's inauguration thus was the first to be held outdoors.

Such pettishness was not characteristic of Clay. For the most part he was faithful to the policy he stated in these words: "I bow to you today because you bow to me."

Calhoun, sometime friend, sometime adversary, said of him: "I don't like Clay. He is a bad man, an imposter, a creator of wicked schemes. I wouldn't speak to him, but by God! I love him." When Calhoun died, Clay delivered a warm eulogy, although he had once said of him, "If that damned raven from South Carolina keeps quiet, I can do something."

Randolph of Virginia was never a friend of the Kentuckian. They even fought a duel, which, though no blood flowed, was described by a connoisseur of such affairs of honor as the "highest-toned" he had ever witnessed. Yet Randolph said, in one of his last public statements: "There is one man, and only one man, who can save the Union. That man is Henry Clay. I know he has the power. I believe he will be found to have the patriotism and firmness equal to the occasion."

46

Clay ended his career as Speaker of the House, an office which it could almost literally be said he created, so greatly had it been transformed, when the Eighteenth Congress adjourned May 3, 1825.

He was only forty-eight years of age. He was known the nation over as an orator and lawmaker, and was far and away the leading man of the West. He was respected by his enemies, loved by his friends, admired generally by men in public life. He had become a President-maker in his final term, for the election of 1824 had been thrown into the House of Representatives and Clay, a loser in the election, had placed his vast influence there behind his old hostile friend, Adams. Clay was appointed Secretary of State, giving Andrew Jackson, who had been high man in the electoral college, the opportunity to cry that a "Corrupt bargain!" had been made between Clay and the new President.

The Kentuckian went on to future glories in the United States and to continued failures—five in all—in his persistent effort to become President. (After one such failure he made the bitter comment, "If there were two Henry Clays, one of them would make the other the President of the United States.") He died June 29, 1852, in Washington.

Political disappointment and personal sorrow matched the triumphs in Clay's life after he left the House of Representatives. All six of his daughters died before he did, and of his five sons one was killed in the Mexican War and another became insane after an accident. In politics, Senator Clay was different from Speaker Clay. As a young man, Clay had chosen the House after brief service in the Senate because he felt it was the branch of Congress that was closer to the people. After leaving the House, he grew in many respects away from the people. He and Jackson were perpetually in conflict, and eventually it was the latter who more accurately represented the sentiments of the expanding, often crude, always vigorous

West. Although he remained forever a hero in Kentucky, Clay turned more and more to sharing the social and economic sentiments of the financiers and capitalists of the Northeast.

Nevertheless, though he could not become President and could not consistently carry the Senate with him as he had carried the House, Clay's later career could be accounted a failure only if measured against the ambitions he held for himself. He was the first great personal force in American politics, the first public figure to attract the deepest affection of the masses of the people.

His gift for bringing together conflicting interests and diverse purposes may well have been the salvation of the United States by buying time for the Union in the years before the Civil War finally came. Clay said, near the end of his life, "If anyone desires to know the leading and paramount object of my public life, the preservation of the Union will furnish him the key." He was speaking of his last great achievement—the Compromise of 1850.

This compromise, which made possible the admission of California to the Union with a Free-State constitution by making some concessions to the South, has been severely criticized as sheer expediency. Yet it probably did save the Union by postponing the Civil War long enough to give the North and West time to merge their strength for the tragic, bloody struggle.

Perhaps Lincoln had that final patriotic effort of a sick and disappointed old man in mind when he spoke feelingly of Henry Clay as "my beau ideal of a statesman."

III

The Czar

THOMAS REED did not set out to be a politician. Born in Portland, Maine, October 18, 1839, young Tom grew up to be a plump boy with a large head and a face that even in his mature years was described as "strangely reminiscent of Raphael's cherub looking out in baby wonder upon a strange and unknown world." As a thoughtful, bookish lad he expected for a time to become a minister.

Reed had joined the Congregational Church in Portland when he was a high-school student, and his religious promise so impressed some of the ladies of the congregation that they raised a sum of money to help pay his way through college—as preparation for entering the ministry. Even when he turned his ambitions to the legal profession—after repaying the church ladies—he still did not think of politics as a career. And when he did thrust a hesitant foot into political waters, he expected only that the experience would advance him in the practice of law with new acquaintanceships to bring him more clients.

1

The college he entered was Bowdoin, a small institution with high standards located at Brunswick, Maine, only twenty-five miles from Portland. The young Reed already displayed the quickness of thought and nimbleness of tongue that were to characterize him in later years. He made a good scholastic record and distinguished himself as an intercollegiate debater. He had many friendly acquaintances but few intimate friends in college; he got along well with his associates without becoming close to them. A classmate later recalled him as "a big, flabby, overgrown boy" who "matured steadily, mentally and physically, while in college." He was graduated in 1860.

He had by now given up the idea of becoming a minister. He taught school in Portland for a year, earning money to pay off his college debts, and began the study of law. Then he went to California, taught school in Stockton for a few months, and resumed his law studies. He was admitted to the bar at San Jose in 1863. Not finding California to his taste, he returned to Maine soon after. "Nature never intended any man to live here, only to dig gold and get himself out of it," he wrote of California, adding tartly, "and shudder in dreams ever afterward."

After service as a Navy paymaster on a boat plying the Mississippi during the closing months of the Civil War, Reed was admitted to the Maine bar in October, 1865. He set up practice in Portland when he was twenty-seven years old. Three years later he took the first step toward his political future.

A professional associate, Nathan Webb, acting without Reed's knowledge, placed the young lawyer's name forward in a Republican caucus as a candidate for the state legislature. Reed resisted the idea of accepting a nomination. He told Webb plainly that he doubted his ability to arouse the voters. He had no desire to become embroiled in politics, nor did he consider that he possessed the talents of a successful politician. For, although amiable and easy in his contacts with other men, he was not a ready mixer.

Eventually, however, he was persuaded that he could be elected and that some political experience would be useful to him in the practice of law. From that reluctant beginning he went on to serve four years in the Maine house of representatives, was elected to the state senate for a term, then became attorney general of the state and held that office for three years. After this sound apprenticeship, he was elected in 1876 to the United States House of Representatives.

Meanwhile, in 1870, he had married Mrs. Susan P. Jones, the widowed daughter of a Portland minister. Through the years, Reed's private life was as serene as his public life was tumultuous. He kept the two as apart as he could, although his wife was so intensely interested in his political activities that he usually tried out his formal speeches on her before delivering them. Mrs. Reed was a woman of tact and sound sense, assets to be of special value when she and her husband reached Washington. Neither she nor her husband cared for the social whirl in the capital. They regarded Portland as their home, and it was in that city rather than in Washington that they centered their social life. When they first went to Washington they lived at a boarding house and, later, in a quiet family hotel. The Reeds had two children, a daughter and a son; the latter died as an infant. Reed was greatly devoted to his family, and all contemporary accounts agree that his home life was an unusually satisfying one.

In those days the regular sessions of Congress began on the first Monday in December, but the Forty-fifth Congress met in special session October 15, 1877. Thomas Brackett Reed was one of the 293 members who took their places in what was currently described as the "Bear Yard" because of the unruly and at times outrageous conduct of many members. The Democrats controlled the House, there being 156 of them to 137 Republicans. The Speaker was Samuel J. Randall of Pennsylvania. The atmosphere was tense and heavy with suspicion.

The suspicion was largely an aftermath of the Tilden-Hayes presidential election of 1876. The popular majority had gone to Governor Samuel J. Tilden of New York, the Democratic candidate, but his 184 electoral votes were one short of a majority. Rutherford B. Hayes of Ohio, the Republican, had 165. Twenty votes were in doubt. Nineteen of the disputed electoral votes came from Florida, Louisiana, and South Carolina, where postwar reconstruction lingered on and vote frauds were common. Each of these states had sent two conflicting sets of election returns to Washington. The remaining electoral vote in dispute came from Oregon, where the eligibility of one of the Republican electors had been challenged and a certificate of election had been issued to his closest Democratic rival. The bitter quarrel threatened the only recently reunited—and forcibly reunited—Union with a renewal of civil war. The threat was ended when an electoral commission created by Congress, voting strictly on party lines, gave all the disputed votes and the election to Hayes. But the bitterness was not dissipated. Southern members continued to charge theft and fraud.

The new member from Maine remembered long afterward that during his first term in the House everybody suspected that everybody else was cheating, or would cheat if given the opportunity. Peace of a sort was kept, he thought, only because of a general fear that if a real fight started it would quickly spread beyond any hope of control.

Reed set no legislative fires ablaze as a freshman in Congress. He presented a few petitions to the House, spoke briefly in support of a proposal to print the report of a monetary commission, brought about passage of a bill authorizing the Secretary of the Treasury to issue a register for, and to change the name of, a schooner operating out of Maine ports. He attracted no special attention. But, seated at his small desk in the Republican grouping to the left of the Speaker's stand, he listened and learned. One of his early observations was that if a member of the House wished to talk and be listened to, "he had better have something to say and know how to say it." Most members, he noted, were not listened to.

His initial committee assignments were not inspiring. He was named to the Committee on Territories and to the Committee on Expenditures in the War Department. Neither afforded any wide opportunities. Before his first term was over, however, he had been appointed a member of the Potter Committee to investigate the 1876 election. This investigation was a bipartisan affair in the sense that each side, the Democrats and the Republicans, sought to secure maximum party advantage from it. In this two-sided effort, the Republicans came out somewhat ahead in the end. By bringing forward convincing evidence that both parties had been guilty of chicanery, they were able to prevent the charge of "stolen election" from being made the overriding issue in the campaign of 1880.

Reed himself benefited considerably from his work on the Potter Committee. The investigation gave him widespread prominence and brought praise from Republican newspapers for the quick-tongued skill he displayed in cross-examining witnesses. The people back in his district were impressed. Reed was re-elected for his second term without difficulty.

The Democrats were again in control of the House and Randall was still Speaker. Randall, brought up in the tough school of Philadelphia politics, was an outstanding parliamentarian as well as a highly knowledgeable politician, and he aroused Reed's interest in parliamentary procedure. The Maine man also admired the diligence with which the Democrat fought for his own party. Reed understood partisanship. He wrote of Randall that "there have been few men with a will more like iron or courage more unfaltering."

Furthermore, Reed was giving close study to the mechanics of the House. He had quickly come to understand that procedure was everything as far as accomplishment in that unruly assembly was concerned. He therefore set out to master the rules of the House and was a lively participant in the debate on a revised code that was brought up during his second term. He was particularly outspoken in opposing an amendment that would have eliminated the "disappearing quorum"—which he, almost singlehandedly, was to kill ten years later. At this time, however, the amendment was withdrawn.

In the 1880 elections the Republicans captured the House as well as retaining the presidency, but a divisive intraparty conflict that had accompanied Garfield's election kept them from making the most of their opportunity. One result of the Republican majority was an upgrading of Reed's committee assignments. He was named to the Committee on the Judiciary, which ranked third among the major House committees, standing below only the Ways and Means and the Appropriations Committees. In addition, he was appointed to the Rules Committee when a member resigned early in the session. He was consolidating his position in the House.

He already had concluded that the rules revision of 1880 provided insufficient lubrication for the creaking House machinery. In the Forty-seventh Congress he was able to cause adoption of an amendment to the rules to provide that, in the case at least of election contests, the Speaker would have the power to suppress filibustering. Such contests, then common in the House, always produced a tremendous amount of time-consuming and partisan talk. Useless talk, too, for the custom was for the majority party to settle such contests in favor of its own, no matter what was said or what evidence was presented.

Adoption of Reed's amendment marked the beginning of his party leadership in the House of Representatives. "Ever after," one commentator has said, "as long as he remained in Congress, his voice gave the word of command." Reed saw his amendment as only a beginning. So did the opposition. If the majority could change the rules to end filibustering in election cases, it logically could go ahead to change the rules to end filibusters in other matters. This was a fearful thought to minority members whose tactics were set in a mold of obstructionism.

Aside from his preoccupation with the rules and procedure of the House, Reed's main interests at this time were free silver and the protective tariff. As a good Republican, he bitterly opposed the first and staunchly upheld the second. Other leading issues during his congressional career included suffrage in the states of the South, civil rights of the former slaves, destruction of the spoils system, and establishment of necessary reforms in the civil service system. Despite the powerful influence he came to exercise with respect to bills having to do with these matters, Reed's name was never associated with any particular legislative measure. But in debate he was in his glory.

He was a commanding figure on the floor of the House. The fat boy of Portland had grown into a giant who stood six feet two inches in height and weighed some 275 pounds. "A big man, physically and mentally," Sam Rayburn was to say of him three-quarters of a century later. "Big head, big brain." Reed could not have been unaware that his sheer massiveness was a valuable asset whenever he heaved himself up from his chair and lumbered toward the well of the House, his large bald head shining, his hazel eyes twinkling. His words came slowly, enunciated with a nasal Maine drawl that his opponents found irritating to an extreme degree, especially when he delivered one satiric thrust after another to drive home his points. He engaged in no gestures, physical or oratorical, but spoke quietly, simply, with erudition and humor—and he spoke devastatingly. It was fortunate for Reed, a member once observed, that dueling had gone out of style among members of Congress, for otherwise his tongue would have provoked innumerable challenges and his mountainous figure would have been a hard target to miss.

Customs having changed, words were flung instead of gauntlets. But the words were not infrequently provocative enough to keep the threat of physical violence lurking over the House chamber. J. Warren Keifer of Ohio, Speaker during the Republican-controlled Forty-seventh Congress, felt it necessary to preside over sessions of the House with a pistol in his pocket so that he could deal with violence if necessary.

After 1880 the size of the House had increased to 332 members, but there had been no corresponding growth in the dignity of the body. Members lounged about the House floor, went to sleep with their feet propped on their desks, read newspapers, even occupied themselves with paring their fingernails during sessions. Some members were often drunk. Tobacco chewing was common. Frank G. Carpenter, fresh-eyed young correspondent for the Cleveland *Leader*, reported to his paper: "Every desk has a spittoon of pink and gold china beside it to catch the filth from the statesman's mouth. It costs at least four hundred dollars a year to care for the spittoons of the House, even though your average congressman often disregards his spittoon and spits on the floor."

There was a requirement that members wear coats, but it was not unusual for a Representative engaged in a heated debate to fling off his jacket in the manner of an evangelist at an old-fashioned camp meeting. This was not, of course, Thomas Reed's style—neither the personal *déshabillé* nor the impassioned, name-calling oratory. He had a corrosive contempt for both, which he did not hesitate to express. As a Washington correspondent for the New York *Times* reported, he delighted "in sticking pins in windbags." Writing to Henry Cabot Lodge after a visit to the Italian Chamber of Deputies in Rome, Reed reported with pleasure that one of the speakers reminded him of a Representative from Alabama. "He kept on and on," Reed explained. "Nobody paid any attention to him, but he never stopped so far as I know. It had such a homelike look, such a familiar sound, that I felt as if I were in my native jungle."

There was no nonpartisan hypocrisy about the gentleman from Maine. "The best system is to have one party govern and the other party watch," he observed on one occasion, "and on general principles I think it would be better for us to govern and the Democrats to watch." In a rough and tumble exchange on the House floor, a New York Democrat declared, "The Republican party drinks a good deal of whiskey clandestinely that we do not know anything about." Reed retorted, "When my friend from New York takes it, it does not remain clandestine very long."

Yet this same Democrat, Samuel S. Cox, earned Reed's ungrudging respect as a man who knew what he was about. "Mr. Cox was not an orator," he said, "hardly a leader, and perhaps not a wit; but in action he was a whole skirmish line, and has covered more movements of the Democratic party and led it out of more parliamentary pitfalls than any of its orators and all of its leaders put together."

When he made a set speech, which was not often, Reed spoke earnestly and with vigor. Despite his high-pitched, rasping voice, he could hold an audience because his speeches bristled with points that no listener dared to miss. But it was in casual repartee that he was most dangerous to the opposition. William M. Springer, Illinois Democrat, was a favorite target for the whiplash of his tongue. Of him Reed once said, "The gentleman never got within a decade of the present in his life and his party surrounds him where he stands." Again, when Springer sought unanimous consent to correct a statement he had made in a speech attacking the Republicans, Reed remarked, "No correction needed. We did not think it was so when it was made."

R. W. Townsend, also of Illinois, once complained that he could not make a five-minute speech against the tariff "but they cry, 'Vote, vote,' and seek to put me down." Reed, sounding somewhat like Mark Twain, commiserated, "It is because you make the same speech every time. It is not the speech we complain of so much as it is the monotony of the thing. We want a change."

Reed would turn his wit on his own constituents if sufficiently provoked. "He tolerated his constituents," Joe Cannon observed, "but I think it is fair to say he did not love them." He had no taste for the errand-boy role in which some members of Congress allowed themselves to be cast. To a group of Maine citizens who asked him to help them obtain a condemned cannon for a soldiers' monument he gave the acrid reply, "I am not in the old junk business."

He was also capable of striking out at members of his own party, as in his comment after James G. Blaine, also of Maine, had been nominated for President in 1884. Asked what he thought of the nomination, Reed replied, "Well, it is a great comfort to think that the wicked politicians were not allowed to pick the candidate, and that the nomination was made by the people. The politicians would have been guided only by a base desire to win." He was never on very good terms with Maine Senators—indeed, he had little esteem for the Senate as an institution—and when his party took over the Executive branch he found his influence on patronage was minimal. Commenting on this, he said, "I had but two enemies in Maine, and one of them [President] Harrison pardoned out of the penitentiary and the other he appointed collector of Portland."

Reed was, as William Allen White, the noted what's-the-matter-with-Kansas editor, wrote of him, "tainted with a certain mugwumpian independence." "Party regularity was a conventional garment with him," White explained, "but not a high priest's robe."

Reed was an unusual kind of politician in other respects. He valued his own privacy; although popular with most of his colleagues and held in deep affection by some, he was rarely to be found in the afterhours hotel-lobby gatherings of the House clan. He preferred to be with his family, and when Congress was not in session he preferred to be in Portland. At his home there he had assembled the largest private library in the state. An avid student of American history and biography, he also read widely in the field of government and kept up with current literary magazines. He admitted to a liking for poetry, which fondness was not a failing of most politicians. He took up the study of French after he was forty and became fairly proficient in both the reading and speaking of that language. His favorite form of entertainment was small dinner parties with close friends. He was not interested in games or sports. His principal exercise was walking, most often alone.

While he could be fitted into no machine-made groove, Reed nevertheless was superbly a politician's politician. Being able to secure re-election term after term without bothering to spoon-feed his constituents, he was left free to maneuver effectively in the arena he had made peculiarly his own—the House of Representatives.

The Democrats regained control of the House in the Forty-eighth Congress and held control for six years. One of the first actions they took was to adopt the rules of the Forty-sixth Congress, thus wiping out the progress Reed had made with his antifilibuster amendment to the rules of the Forty-seventh.

Reed protested, "We are authorized by the Constitution of the United States to make rules, not for the hindrance of business, but for the transaction of the business of the House and of the country." But his protest was in vain.

A basic conflict in governmental philosophy was involved. Reed held that the rules should be drawn to enable the House to function and to meet what he saw as its urgent responsibilities in a changing world. John G. Carlisle of Kentucky, the new Speaker, and his lieutenants, on the other hand, were traditionalists who, in Reed's view, considered the safest course was to do nothing.

Even though he saw Carlisle as a man of ability, "the ablest man they have on that side of the House," Reed declared that Carlisle was made ineffective by his rigid adherence to outworn modes of procedure and his resistance to reforming the House rules. "No Speaker could do better," said Reed, "with his hands tied by the rules we are working under." Even Randall, for whom he had great respect and who, because of his tariff views, had not been named Speaker again, "had passed his life in the minority, trying to prevent things from being done," Reed charged, "and was therefore more anxious that the new machine should have perfect back motion than that it should have forward movement."

The effort "to prevent things from being done" was successful, on the whole. As the end of the session approached, the Democrats had to exert hard pressure to get action on the necessary appropriation bills and at least a few other measures. Most of the session's proposals for legislation were caught in a hopeless log jam. "We undertake to run Niagara through a quill," Reed remarked caustically. He had figured out, he announced, that under its existing rules the House could transact only 8 per cent of its business.

From the beginning of the Forty-eighth Congress to its end, Reed had kept up a constant agitation for changes in the rules. There was a feeling in the House that he had made some headway. Even Speaker Carlisle, in his end-of-the-session speech, dwelt painfully on the legislative congestion and tacitly admitted that some procedural changes might be needed. A few revisions were made in the following Congress, but they were not deep-rooted—only expedients hopefully designed to lighten the cumulative pressure. The carefully patterned design advocated by Reed was not yet in evidence. To his own question about the House Democrats—"Are they but an organized 'No'?" —he would still have to give an affirmative answer.

The Maine Representative was the Republican nominee for Speaker in the Forty-ninth Congress, which assembled in December, 1885. The Democrats still had a majority in the House and Carlisle again became Speaker, but Reed's nomination made him the titular leader of his party in the House. He retained that place until his retirement from Congress fourteen years later.

He promptly resumed his attack on the House rules, declaring them to be an outrage against the principle of government by majority. "The only way to do business inside the rules is to suspend the rules," he told the House. "The object of the rules appears to be to prevent the transaction of business." But he got nowhere in that Congress or in the one that followed.

In this latter Congress, the Fiftieth, with the House controlled by the Democrats and the Senate by the Republicans, the legislative process came close to breaking down. Even the most routine measures were passed only with the greatest difficulty. Filibusters, one after another, occupied the time of the House and drew the by no means favorable attention of the country. The press described what was going on as "filibustering run mad." In one instance, a single member, James B. Weaver of Iowa (who was to be the Populist candidate for President in 1892), was successful in keeping the House from conducting any business whatever for a period of almost two weeks.

The Rules Committee, with Carlisle as chairman, remained completely dormant throughout this Congress. All Republicans in the House signed a petition to the Speaker requesting him to call a meeting of his committee and make a report, but the petition was ignored.

In this Congress, Reed's biographer, William A. Robinson, later wrote, "The House of Representatives reached the nadir of ineffectiveness. Its exhibitions of helplessness and ineptitude under existing rules far surpassed any previous displays of the sort." When the session ended, the Washington *Post* editorially attributed its do-nothing record to the "un-Democratic, un-Republican, and un-American rules of the House of Representatives."

The Republicans took everything in the election of November, 1888. General Benjamin Harrison was elected President. His party kept control of the Senate and gained a majority—although of only eight members—in the House. Once again the presidency and both houses of Congress were in the charge of the same party.

In the caucus of Republican members of the House that was held prior to the opening session of the Fifty-first Congress, Reed was nominated for Speaker. In the caucus he received eighty-five votes to thirty-eight for William McKinley of Ohio and nineteen for Joseph Cannon of Illinois; two other candidates divided twenty-four votes between them. The choice of the caucus became Speaker on December 2, 1889. A quorum of the House consisted of 166 members on the day of Reed's election. He received exactly that number of votes; Carlisle received 154.

The excruciatingly narrow Republican majority was cut down a bit more by the death of one of the Representatives on that side of the aisle. The new Speaker knew that rarely would as many Republicans be present in the House as on opening day. His paramount problem would be to get a quorum.

From the First Congress the practice had been to determine whether a quorum existed simply by calling the roll. If any member, even though present, remained silent during a roll-call vote, he was not counted for the purpose of establishing

61

a quorum—thus, the "disappearing" quorum. Under such conditions, as Reed was well aware, the Democratic minority could prevent not merely the passage but even the consideration of any legislation to which they were opposed. They needed only to make the point that a quorum was not present. That they could do at will and thus effectively stall House action.

Earlier that year, in an article for *Century* magazine, Reed had written: "Our government is founded on the doctrine that if 100 think one way and 101 think the other, the 101 are right. It is the old doctrine that the majority must govern. Indeed, you have no choice. If the majority do not govern, the minority will; and if the tyranny of the majority is hard, the tyranny of the minority is unendurable. The rules, then, ought to be so arranged as to facilitate the action of the majority."

The fact remained that the rules were not arranged that way. The division of strength was so nearly equal that, using the filibuster as a parliamentary weapon, the Democrats could negate any legislative effort the Republicans might make.

Reed explained his concept of the speakership in his opening speech to the House: "Under our system of government as it has developed, the responsibilities and duties of this office are both political and parliamentary. So far as the duties are political, I sincerely hope they may be performed with a proper sense of what is due to the people of this whole country. So far as they are parliamentary, I hope with equal sincerity that they may be performed with a proper sense of what is due to both sides of this chamber."

That was the substance of his brief formal address. He added more two weeks after the session had opened. The Democratic members may have thought the Speaker was making a political *bon mot* when he announced that he expected to look out for the interests of the Republican Party from the Chair and that the Democrats would have to take care of themselves. But the man from Maine was not joking. He meant for the majority to rule.

2

On January 29, 1890, eight weeks after the convening of the Fifty-first Congress, an election contest involving two obscure West Virginia gentlemen named Jackson and Smith was called up for consideration in the House. There was no real question about how the House would vote to settle the contest. The Republicans would give the seat to the candidate of their own party, thus enhancing by one their razor-edge majority. But it was a formality that had to be performed—if the Democratic minority would permit the machinery of the House to function.

The Democrats had no intention of doing that if they could prevent it. In any case, they could be counted on to forestall action for as long as possible. The yeas and nays were demanded on the question of whether the contest should be considered by the House. On the roll call, 161 members voted affirmatively, two voted against consideration, and 165 members—including some who a few moments before had joined in demanding the roll-call vote—were recorded as not voting.

The ayes seemed to have it, the Speaker announced.

Charles F. Crisp, the skilled Democratic parliamentarian from Georgia, sprang to his feet to raise the point that a quorum was not present. That was the method by which the Democrats had determined to make certain the Republican-dominated Fifty-first would be a do-nothing Congress. The system had been foolproof in the past, for Speaker Carlisle had repeatedly ruled that when the point of "no quorum" was raised it could be met only by a roll call to demonstrate whether or not a voting quorum was present.

Reed, never more benign, ignored Crisp's shouts of "No quorum."

"The Chair directs the clerk," he said, his nasal voice calm, "to record the names of the following members present and refusing to vote."

Looking over the Democrats present, he then proceeded to call the names of a number, including Carlisle and other leaders

of the party, who had refrained from voting on the consideration question.

The House erupted. The uproar was as violent as any ever
seen in that often tempestuous body. Each time the Speaker
called another name to add to the list that would make up a
quorum, new catcalls were shouted, more fists shaken passion-
ately in the air.

When William P. Breckinridge of Kentucky heard his name
called, he stood in the aisle and bellowed, "I deny the power of
the Speaker and denounce it as revolutionary."

The Democrats in the chamber cheered wildly. Reed waited
for the noise to subside, and then continued to call names for
the clerk to list.

Richard P. Bland of Missouri, failing in his attempt to gain
recognition from the Chair, cried in anger, "I am responsible
to my constituents for the way in which I vote, and not to the
Speaker of the House."

The Speaker ignored him and proceeded.

Barnes Compton of Maryland, raising his voice above the
raucous clamor of his colleagues, stated his complaint in dignified terms: "I protest against the conduct of the Chair in calling
my name."

Reed went ahead with the business of calling more names.

Walter Hayes of Iowa bawled, "I appeal from any decision—
any decision—so far as I am concerned."

Reed called the names of more members.

By the time he reached J. B. McCreary of Kentucky, that
gentleman had been able to collect his faculties sufficiently to
offer what under the circumstances was a formal statement of
protest: "I deny your right, Mr. Speaker, to count me as present,
and I desire to read from the parliamentary law on that
subject."

The serene Buddha at the Speaker's stand directed his inno-
cent gaze toward the protester. "The Chair is making a statement of fact that the gentleman from Kentucky is present," he
drawled. "Does he deny it?"

Laughter and applause came from the Republican side of the chamber, groans and imprecations from the Democrats. And the count went on until Reed had called off the names of forty-one of the nonvoting members present in the chamber. Then he coolly announced that a quorum was *in fact* present and that the resolution to consider the election contest had been passed.

He elaborated: "There is a provision in the Constitution which declares that the House may establish rules for compelling the attendance of members. If members can be present and refuse to exercise their functions and cannot be counted as a quorum, that provision would seem to be entirely nugatory. Inasmuch as the Constitution only provides for their attendance, that attendance is enough. If more was needed, the Constitution would have provided for more.

"The Chair thereupon rules," Reed concluded, "that there is a quorum present within the meaning of the Constitution."

He also pointed out, not without disingenuousness, that, having treated the quorum question in "an orderly fashion," he was subject under the rules to being overruled by the House on an appeal from his decision. Crisp immediately appealed from the ruling. He and Carlisle led the Democrats in a savage onslaught against the Speaker's departure from the traditional practice of the House. The appeal was finally laid on the table. Significantly, this was done by a majority not of the whole House but of the counted quorum.

Reed had won the first skirmish, but the fight was far from over. Representatives left the Capitol late that evening in a high state of excitement, the Democrats furiously resolved to take up the battle again on the following day. Their first attack came in the form of a refusal to vote on the routine question of approving the House Journal for the previous day. Reed again counted members present but not voting and ruled that a quorum was present.

William M. Springer appealed the decision. Reed refused to entertain the appeal on the ground that the House had decided that question the day before and there was no value in traveling the same road again. Once more the House was the scene of a near riot. Members rushed about the floor, waving their arms and bawling out epithets against the Speaker. "Czar!" "Despot!" "Tyrant!" Those were among the names he was called that day.

When Springer insisted upon his right to be heard on his point of order that no quorum had voted, Reed refused to recognize him.

"The gentleman from Illinois will take his seat," he ordered.

"The gentleman from Illinois will take his seat or not as he chooses," Springer bellowed. "There are no rules under which I can be called on to take my seat, and I can stand up here if I desire."

He could stand as long as he wished, but still the Speaker would not recognize him.

The brawl continued throughout the afternoon and the following day. It was a three-day fight that made substantial and lasting changes in the House of Representatives. Time after time the Democrats sat silent as their names were reached on roll calls. Time after time the weary, patient, determined man in the Chair took the roll from the clerk and instructed him to call the names of Democrats who were in the chamber but had not voted. Each announcement that the motion was agreed to and that a quorum was present brought renewed roars from the Democrats.

Near the end, realizing that they were getting nowhere with their protests, members of the recalcitrant minority began trying to escape the eye of the quorum-counting Speaker by lurking under their desks, dodging behind screens, or bolting for the exits. In their frenzy, many lost all sense of official or even personal dignity. It was a mob scene. Some individuals actually suffered minor physical injuries in their single-minded scramble to get out of Reed's sight.

At one point the Speaker ordered the doors locked. A Texas Representative, Constantine Buckley Kilgore, set on leaving the hall, kicked out the panels of a door leading into the lobby.

The door crashed open with some damage to the nose of Reed's dignified Maine colleague, Nelson Dingley, who had been standing outside. Kilgore made his exit and, thanks to newspaper correspondents looking for sidelight stories on the great quorum fight, was known thereafter as "Kicking Buck." He became quite a tourist attraction.

The large man in the Speaker's chair remained calm and outwardly unmoved throughout the pandemonium, "not for an instant losing his presence of mind," as the New York *Tribune* admiringly reported. His patience seemed without limit. He rose above insult and abuse, making his rulings in an unemotional voice somewhat higher and more nasal than usual. It was an exhibition of outstanding personal courage and iron self-control. Later his friend Henry Cabot Lodge commented: "Although he was capable of anger and strongly combative, I never saw his good nature fail, or his ready wit turn, as it might well have done, to anger and fierce denunciation." The Speaker held back any rage he felt for the confines of his private office and the companionship of two or three close friends.

Afterwards, according to Robinson, Reed said that during these sessions the House often reminded him of "a wild beast leaping toward the rostrum as far as its chain permitted, but never quite breaking loose."

Among the most vociferous and agitated Democrats was William B. Bynum of Indiana, who, denouncing "the outrageous and damnable ruling of the Chair," shouted that he did not propose "to be silenced or gagged on this floor." "In the language of the immortal Emmet," the gentleman from Indiana cried, "we propose to dispute every inch of ground, burn every blade of grass, and the last entrenchment of liberty shall be our graves."

Reed met this grandiloquent quotation from an Irish rebel with aplomb. Banging his gavel until a semblance of order was restored, he remarked mildly, "The House will not allow itself to be deceived by epithets. No man can describe the action and judgment of this Chair in language which will endure unless that description be true."

He took advantage of the occasion to make a clear statement of the situation as he saw it. "Whenever it becomes apparent," he told the House, "that the ordinary and proper parliamentary methods are being used solely for purposes of delay and obstruction; when members break in an unprecedented way over the rules in regard to the reading of the Journal; when a gentleman steps down to the front, amid the applause of his associates on the floor, and announces that it is his intention to make opposition in every direction, it then becomes apparent to the House and to the country what the purpose is. It is then the duty of the occupant of the Speaker's chair to take, under parliamentary law, the proper course with regard to such matters."

Once again he turned to the familiar task of counting a quorum on the question of laying on the table the appeal from his decision. He refused to accept a motion to adjourn. The motion was dilatory, he ruled.

John Dalzell of Pennsylvania, a Reed lieutenant, brought up the by now almost forgotten election case. Crisp's automatic effort to revive the question of consideration was ruled out of order, the Speaker declined to entertain an appeal from the decision, and debate finally began on the momentous question of whether Smith or Jackson should be seated as a Representative from West Virginia. On February 2, 1891, Smith, the Republican, was seated by a vote of one more than a quorum.

Reed had won. It was a fight that he could have lost at any moment by the desertion to the other side of no more than a handful of Republicans. But his party stayed with him to a man, although initially some of the Republican members were as taken aback by the Speaker's tactics as the Democrats had been. Reed was so determined on his course that he had told Elihu Root, in advance of his ruling, that if his party failed to support him he would resign the speakership and his seat in the House. That turned out not to be necessary.

The time had come for his next momentous step.

Up to this point in the session, Reed had not followed the

usual custom of having the rules of the preceding House adopted provisionally. He had conducted business under the more elastic code of general parliamentary law. Now he was prepared for the adoption of the formal rules. He had been at work revising them for several weeks. The report of the Committee on Rules actually had been in his desk the day the quorum-counting fight started. The other two Republican members of the committee were McKinley and Cannon, but the report was largely the Speaker's own creation. The last revision of the rules, which had been made in 1880, had been a product of cooperative effort, but these were the "Reed Rules"—and Reed's they were.

The new code kept unchanged more than half the rules of the Fiftieth Congress and made changes only in technical details in a number of others. But, in spite of the warning implicit in Reed's rulings from the Chair since the session opened, the House was thoroughly shaken by the few important changes that were made.

The session had been only a few weeks old when the Speaker ruled that a motion to adjourn, traditionally regarded as highly privileged, was dilatory and therefore unacceptable. Now, in the proposed new code, dilatory motions were attacked head on. The old rules provided that a motion to fix the day on which the House should adjourn, a motion to adjourn, and a motion to take a recess were always in order. A roll call required about thirty minutes. So a single member, by alternating and repeating privileged motions, could keep the House from doing anything. Reed's rules not only eliminated the privileged motions but also added a new clause, stating flatly that "no dilatory motion shall be entertained by the Speaker." The second great change was the provision that members present but not voting could be counted as a part of the quorum. This provision was strengthened by a rule authorizing the Speaker to order that absent members be arrested and brought before the House and there counted as present for the purpose of constituting a quorum.

Other changes, although they caused less controversy, were

of fundamental importance. One new rule provided that a hundred members would constitute a quorum in the Committee of the Whole, a change long needed because of the vast increase in the volume of congressional business. The Committee of the Whole also was given the power to close debate on any action or paragraph of a bill under consideration, another checkrein on obstructionist tactics. The Reed Rules further provided for readjustments in the order of business that would enable the House to move freely from one legislative calendar to another and from the House to the Committee of the Whole. This gave needed flexibility to House procedure.

Democratic members greeted the report of the Rules Committee with a renewed outburst of bitter criticism. "Despoiler of the Constitution" and "assassin of democratic government" were two of the kindlier accusations made against the author of the revised code.

Reed was not swayed by such attention from the opposition. "The Democratic Party wants no legislation," he observed sardonically. "It is not charged with the progress of the world. All the Southern men who control the party want or ask for is to be let alone. When the Republican party comes into power it has work to do. If that action can be prevented, what more should the Southern Democrats desire? Hence all their plans, whether in power or out of power, are centered on obstruction."

The Reed Rules were adopted February 14, 1890, by a vote of 161 to 144, with twenty-three members not voting. There was not, on this occasion, any disappearing quorum. The House of Representatives would never be the same again.

3

When Tom Reed was a youngster in Portland, his friends often commented that he might become a great man some day if only he were not so lazy. He was by nature "inclined to rest rather than work," Hubert Bruce Fuller wrote of Reed in his book, *The Speakers of the House;* but he could be industrious, and he chose to be industrious as Speaker of the House. He needed to be. He was responsible for a very large amount of everyday business which, at his hopelessly cluttered desk, he handled grumblingly but with close attention to the essential detail involving innumerable bills and resolutions. He always informed himself on what was happening in the House and in its committees.

The grumbling stopped, of course, when the matter at hand involved parliamentary procedure necessary to carry out his program. This was the part of his job that Reed especially liked. He provided himself with effective weapons by radically reshaping the functions of the Committee on Rules. In the past this committee had little to do except recommend rules for the House at the beginning of each session. Reed turned it into a power vehicle of magnitude by making the Committee on Rules in effect the steering committee of the majority party in the House. He accomplished this by developing a new legislative concept—the special rule. Under his system, one that has prevailed since then, the Rules Committee wrote a specific rule for the floor management of a specific bill. The special rule set the time allowed for floor debate and, if the committee so decided, limited the amendments that could be offered to the bill.

Every special rule was written, naturally, by a majority of the five-man committee. The Speaker, chairman of the committee and designator of the other members, controlled the majority. Thus the Speaker had virtually unlimited authority over floor action. It was a system that, added to the new code of rules, could bring the House close indeed to being a one-man show.

In practice, Reed would confer with McKinley and Cannon, the other two Republican members of the committee, as to how a special rule on a given bill should be written. Then the Speaker would send for the two minority members, James G. Blount of Georgia and Benton McMillin of Tennessee, and tell them what had been determined.

"Gentlemen," he would say, smilingly benevolent, "we have

decided to perpetrate the following outrage."

"He never tried to catch us napping," McMillin recalled, "but the Committee on Rules was never a debating society in which Blount and I took part. No, sir!"

The new Speaker had become literally the master of the House. He was, said a Democratic member, "the mentor of the Republicans and the tormentor of the Democrats." Another denounced him for "sitting in the chair with his feet on the neck of the Republican party." Reed hardly bothered to use diplomacy and probably was incapable of using political wiles. Now he had the House rules on his side. He re-enforced them with the force of his will and with the logic that the Fifty-first Congress had been given a popular mandate to legislate.

"We have got to do practical business in this House," he argued. "Statesmanship does not consist in doing the best thing, but in doing the best possible thing. We have got to do what the resources of this country and, above all, the sentiment of the country will support and sustain."

Newspaper cartoonists had a happy time picturing the Speaker as "Czar Reed." Presiding over the sessions of the House, he did indeed have the appearance of an imperial figure, albeit in that summer of 1890 a somewhat bedraggled one. Fashion called for men to wear soft flannel shirts and, in lieu of vests, sashes of silk or wool. The Washington *Post* expressed the opinion that, despite his domination of the House, Reed had "not yet acquired the self-confidence which ought to accompany the wearing of a flannel shirt."

"His coat is drawn up over his breast and fastened by the two upper buttons," the *Post* reported. "It looks as though he was ashamed and as if he desired to hide as much of his shirt as possible." As for the sash: "The Speaker looks like an honest rutabaga wound in a black ribbon." Reed's huge body and massive head lent themselves readily to caricature. In a stock cartoon portrayal, he would be shown wearing an ornate crown and wielding a scepter across the shoulders of a group of cowed Representatives.

But there was more to ruling the House than that. Reed had an intimate knowledge of most members on both sides of the aisle. He knew their strengths and their weaknesses and, with an endless flow of information coming to him from his closest lieutenants, he had the "feel of the House" in the highest degree. Besides, the majority was solidly behind him. Crisp despairingly complained, "The unquestioning loyalty of the Republican following to Reed reminds me of the Hindu who, kneeling in prayer before his idol, consoled himself with the idea that though his god was ugly he knew it was great."

Reed did not coddle his fellow Republicans any more than he had ever coddled his constituents in Maine. "You are too big a fool to lead, and you haven't got sense enough to follow," he cruelly told a colleague who had failed in his responsibility to guide a certain bill through the House. Another member, his bill killed by an objection from Cannon, plaintively asked why he had objected. Cannon told him the Speaker had asked him to object. The angry member then went to the Speaker, demanding, "What do you mean by granting me recognition and then getting Cannon to kill my bill?" Reed replied casually, "To get rid of you."

His sharpest shafts continued to be aimed at the opposition party—in and out of the House of Representatives. He was once the principal speaker at a Maine gathering that included a large number of Democrats. Reed, aware that it was a bipartisan audience, opened his address by saying, "If a photographic snapshot could be taken of the Democrats at any time or any place it would reveal them in the act of doing some mean, low-lived and contemptible thing." He was interrupted by wholehearted boos and jeers from the Democratic section of his audience. "There," said Reed, smiling angelically, "I told you so."

He kept up a steady barrage against the opposition on the House floor. Commenting on the re-election chances of "Kicking Buck" Kilgore, he remarked, "Oh, the gentleman from Texas is safe. His district is Democratic naturally. The common school system does not prevail there." To another Lone Star State member, Roger Q. Mills, he said, "The gentleman does not mean to be believed when he says the Republican party is for free whiskey, because he knows there would not be enough Democrats left to make up the electoral ticket in half the states of the Union if they had confidence in his statement." Sarcastically apologizing for his inability "to equal the volume of voice" shown by a New York Democrat, Reed added, "That is only equaled in this world by the volume of things with which he is not acquainted." Of two particularly long-winded colleagues he said, "They never open up their mouths without subtracting from the sum of human knowledge." Asked by a friend his opinion of another member, Reed drawled, "Well, he is a first-rate fellow and I like him very much. But the trouble with him is that he fails to realize his true relation to the stellar universe."

Despite his authoritarian rule and the sharpness of his tongue, the Speaker could be markedly thoughtful and considerate of individuals. Rodney Wallace of Massachusetts called him "one of the most benevolent and kindly men in assisting new legislators." Champ Clark, later to be Speaker himself, spoke of his debt to Reed "for kindness, promotion, and commendation." Significantly, Reed was immensely popular among House employees.

Still he was "The Czar" and conducted himself accordingly. One time he overruled a point of order made by a Democratic member, only to have the dissenter approach him with his little book on parliamentary procedure—the Reed Rules, no less—and point out that there the Speaker had taken a different position. Reed gave a negligent glance at the passage indicated by the Representative. "Oh," he said, solemn-faced, "the *book* is wrong."

During one of the stormy sessions an opponent demanded, "What becomes of the rights of the minority?" Reed retorted happily, "The right of the minority is to draw its salaries and its function is to make a quorum."

In a more serious vein, he gave this explanation of his view of how the legislation function should be performed: "The whole matter is very simple. You have a representative body to legislate for a great country. Many thousands of bills are introduced at each session. If the House worked day and night it could not give intelligent consideration to one half of these matters. In practice it is found impossible to act upon one tenth of them. What then shall we do? Shall there be no legislation because not all can be done that should be done? If some must be favored for consideration, who shall select these? The committees? Yes; but there are many committees, all pressing for legislation which they deem important, and the House has only so much time at its disposal. In order that anything like attention to the most important interests shall be given, there must be a process of selection. That work cannot well be given over. The Speaker alone is responsible to the entire House. He must aim, of course, to carry out the desires of the committees and should he act in an arbitrary or unfair way, he would be very quickly brought to book by them. He cannot exist without their support."

Clearly, while taking full advantages of the entertainment possibilities of all the fun and shouting, Reed was utterly serious about his duties as Speaker. The Fifty-first Congress enacted, according to one commentator, more measures of public importance than any since the first Civil War Congress in 1861. Among the legislation passed were the Sherman Purchase Act and the McKinley Tariff Act. The latter is credited by political historians with having been an important factor in the defeat of the Republicans in the 1890 congressional elections and, conversely, in the nomination and election two years later of its putative author as President. The attention, favorable and unfavorable, focused on the act gave McKinley national prominence, making it easier for Mark Hanna to arrange his nomination in the 1896 Republican convention.

Much of the legislation passed in Reed's first term as Speaker was partisan. Appropriations reached an all-time high, giving the Democrats "the billion dollar Congress" as a campaign charge. Reed tried to use the term to his own party's advantage, retorting, "This is a billion dollar country." But the people of the country did not feel that rich. On Election Day the Democrats took over the House by a landslide.

On the day the Fifty-first Congress adjourned, the Democrats had revenge of a sort for all they had endured at the hands of their "tormentor." As usual, a resolution expressing thanks to the Speaker for his services was offered just before adjournment. Such a resolution customarily was passed without dissent, but this time the Democrats voted against it.

In his response to the contested resolution, Reed offered no apologies for his conduct as Speaker. Nor did he offer any witticisms.

"What we have done here is in large manner political," he stated. "Whatever is political rouses the sternest, the most turbulent, the most unforgiving passions of the human race. Political action can never be justly judged from a near standpoint. Time and distance are needed for a ripe judgment and the verdict of history is the only verdict worth recording." He thought the verdict of history would be not unfavorable, for "having demonstrated to the people that those who have been elected to do their will can do it, henceforth excuses will not be taken for performance; and government by the people will be stronger in the land."

The Fifty-second Congress contained 231 Democrats, only 88 Republicans, and 14 Populists. The Democrats, meeting in caucus, had some difficulty in choosing their Speaker, but Crisp was eventually nominated on the thirtieth ballot. Reed dropped back to his former position of minority leader. Members of the minority in this Congress, he reported, "behaved with gentleness and modesty, partly because they were very good men and partly because there were very few of them." As for the Democrats, he held that they continued to cling to their old practice of preferring to do nothing. "I tell you, gentlemen," he twitted, "it is a course of that sort, pursued for a century, that has made the House come to be regarded as the coward center of the United States."

The Democrats, long before the session started, had expressed their determination to do away with the Reed Rules. And so they did. The new code, not adopted until the third month of the session, was the old rules of the Fiftieth Congress with some minor modifications. Filibustering again was permitted. In view of the overwhelming Democratic majority, the disappearing quorum was not a problem. The Democrats themselves, looking forward to the next election, concentrated on mending political fences. In summing up the first session, Reed wrote that the House "led a gelatinous existence, the scorn of all vertebrate animals." The Democratic leadership, he gibed, was making certain that "the party should enter the next election unencumbered by principles."

In the Fifty-third Congress, with Crisp again in the Speaker's chair, Reed enjoyed the satisfaction of seeing his quorum-counting rule adopted by the Democratic majority. The Republicans, having greatly increased their strength in the House, were no longer so well behaved. Reed led them in the tactics of obstruction which had caused him first to favor the rule. He really showed the Democrats how to filibuster, and under his leadership Republican members declined to vote. The House was held in deadlock for weeks.

Crisp remarked plaintively, "The leader that they follow has one great thought, one great idea in his mind, and that is to force this side to count a quorum." He was able to do it, too, when on April 17, 1894, the Democrats gave up. A new rule permitting the counting of a quorum was approved by a vote of 213 to 47, with 93 members not voting. A present instead of a voting quorum has been a rule of the House ever since.

The Republicans had a large majority in the Fifty-fourth Congress and Reed was elected Speaker over Crisp by a vote of 240 to 95. Since the Democratic Cleveland was in the White House, the Speaker was the official head of his party in the entire country.

77

Samuel McCall, in his biography of the Speaker, wrote of Reed in this period: "Out of the vituperation and calumny of his first speakership and the hard and continuous fighting as minority leader in the next two Congresses, he had emerged into smooth water, with an enormous majority behind him, vindicated by the country and vindicated, too, by his political opponents in that part of his official conduct which they had most violently assailed. He took a placid enjoyment in presiding over the House, and his manner was much like that of a benevolent teacher."

It was not that easy, but there was no denying that a considerable change had taken place. First, the Speaker now was surrounded by political friends instead of being overwhelmed by political antagonists. Second, the state of Maine had come into her own. The Maine delegation in the House consisted of only four men, but each of them had seen long service and each occupied a powerful position: Reed was Speaker and chairman of the Rules Committee; Nelson Dingley was chairman of the potent Ways and Means Committee and majority floor leader as well; Charles Boutelle was chairman of the Naval Affairs Committee; and Seth Milliken was chairman of the Public Buildings Committee.

The floor leader was an especially close friend of the Speaker. Dingley, a man of high principles and serious mien ("Always looked like a man who had just lost his best and dearest friend," said Cannon), was a former governor of Maine and he and Reed had long worked together. Reed regarded him with great affection but could never resist teasing his friend, who was a strong temperance advocate and prominent in the affairs of the Congregational Church. The Speaker once approached Dingley while he was working with other members of the Ways and Means Committee and, staring thoughtfully into his face, said, "Dingley, you are too good. There's such a thing as average goodness, and you have run it up so high in this Congress that I know six members who lay their ruin to your door for making it so hard to bring the average down to the proper level."

Cannon told the story of a dinner he attended along with Reed, Dingley, and a few others. Reed liked wine with his dinner, but the host was a Maine temperance man and no wine appeared. "In those days," Cannon related, "halfway through dinner there was always served what was known as a Roman punch, which was simply a water ice flavored with whiskey, rum, or a cordial. When the Roman punch came, Reed fell upon it avidly, but Dingley, sitting across the table, tasted it gingerly, again approached it cautiously, then laid his spoon down and said in a mournful voice with his sorrowful countenance, 'Tom, there's rum in that,' and his words and tone were a reproach to move the deepest sinner. Reed leisurely finished his punch and, turning to the table, drawled out, 'That's the difference between Nelson and me. He knows rum the moment he tastes it, but I had to finish mine before I discovered it!' "

Reed's feeling toward Dingley was kindly even when he was teasing him, for he knew that his friend was utterly sincere in his goodness. With those he suspected of hypocrisy he was less tolerant. Joseph H. Choate, future Ambassador to the Court of St. James's, once remarked of himself in a small group where Reed was present that he had lived "a clean and decent life," had never played cards, drunk whiskey, or chewed tobacco. "Lord," said Senator Edward Wolcott of Colorado, "I wish I could say that."

"Why don't you say it?" Reed returned pleasantly. "Choate did."

During this period Reed was frequently suggested as a possibility for the Senate, but he was not interested. His opinion of the Senate was not high. It was, he once said, "a place where good Representatives go when they die." He wrote an unpublished fantasy purporting to be "A History of the United States, Published in 1940," in which he told of a change in the Constitution providing that the President should be chosen by the Senate from its own membership. When the ballots were counted, it turned out that each Senator had received one vote. "Never until that moment," Reed wrote, "had the people realized that . . . the Senate of the United States was one level mass of wisdom and virtue, perfect in all its parts, and radiant from North to South with that light of intelligence which never shone on sea or shore."

While he had no desire to be a Senator, Reed strongly hoped to be the Republican nominee for President in 1896. To a friend who asked whether he expected to get the nomination he replied, "They might do worse and they probably will."

He never had a chance. Skilled though he was at parliamentary infighting in the House, he was hardly a politician at all in the "practical" sense of the word, and no doubt would have scorned to be one. He held the highest place in Congress, but he had no national following, no organization of state and precinct workers in the political arena. Furthermore, he was not willing to make either promises or commitments. To add to these handicaps, Western Republicans had told Mark Hanna that Reed was not one of them, that he thought he was their superior, that he was, in short, "stuck up." Hanna, whose distinctions included that of being the first to describe Republican policy as "stand pat," hastened to spread the word as part of his own campaign to secure the nomination for McKinley.

Even when he was thinking of himself as a candidate for the presidential nomination, Reed hardly acted like a candidate. Members of the House who sought special favor from the Speaker were given short shrift. One who asked for a promise of recognition to bring up a private bill was told bluntly, "The bill will not be allowed to come up, even with that Reed button on your coat." His friend, Cannon, reported sorrowfully, "He does not stop to think about his candidacy at all. If he did, he would not day after day deny the appeals of members who say they must have certain appropriations or they cannot be re-elected, and cannot cultivate in their districts any sentiment favorable to the nomination of Mr. Reed."

McKinley was nominated, of course, and the election gave the Republicans both the presidency and a comfortable majority in Congress. And the House again named Reed as Speaker.

Fortunately for the new President, Reed was strictly loyal to the party. Moreover, he favored in principle a full restoration of the protective tariff system, which was a matter of pressing concern to the McKinley Administration. He thought little of McKinley himself, characterizing him as having "the backbone of a chocolate eclair."

"If Tom Reed were several sizes smaller in statesmanship," commented the Washington *Post*, "he would step to one side and allow the pork-hunting Congressmen to pile up some very embarrassing legislation for the McKinley Administration to wrestle with." But there was no possibility that Republican Reed of Maine would do anything like that.

He gave the necessary support to appropriation bills and other measures called for by the Spanish-American War, although he felt that war could have been avoided by a little less emotional jingoism and a little more intelligence in dealing with the issues involved. As the war proceeded, he was depressed by the inept way in which it was conducted and was embittered by the consequent suffering of American troops. Then he found himself completely at odds with his party colleagues on the question of annexing Hawaii to the United States.

Despite his frequent flippancy and his at least occasional cynicism, Reed was an American who so loved his country that any national departure from dignity or honor was anathema to him. He believed with the utmost seriousness in the tenets stated in the Declaration of Independence. He held a strong conviction that the people of any country had a right to self-determination and self-government. Years before the Hawaiian annexation was proposed he had said, "The best government of which a people is capable is a government which they establish for themselves. With all its imperfections, with all its shortcomings, it is always better adapted to them than any other government, even though invented by wiser men."

Yet, in this matter, he was not in accord with most of the members of the House, including members of his own party.

81

In the past, when accused of tyranny in his conduct of the speakership, his reply had been, "The approval of the House is the very breath in the nostrils of the Speaker." Now he lacked that approval. Robinson wrote, "Unwilling to break with the party which he had served so long and equally unwilling to accept its new position, he was being steadily forced into a position of isolation."

During much of his last term as Speaker he was a lonely figure. On pleasant days he often walked to the Capitol, his huge form lumbering along Pennsylvania Avenue in solitary grandeur. He had once told a friend that he could not abide being isolated, that he liked to be where he could rub elbows with people. But now he chose, often, to be alone.

He retained the respect of the House and his power over it. He would have been able, had he chosen, to do much to obstruct the war effort. He was still "The Czar." From the other side of the Capitol came a bitter, adjective-laden complaint from a member of the Senate: "We have a horrible example before us constantly, like a nightmare, in another end of the Capitol building, where one man transacts the business of 357, which absolutely paralyzes one branch of Congress, a thing which, to my way of thinking, is an absolute, positive, inexcusable, bold, and open disgrace to the American people." But Reed could hardly be expected to feel concern about what a mere Senator said of him.

He used his power to delay consideration of the Hawaiian annexation resolution until he was finally dissuaded by his old friend, Dingley, who knew that public sentiment and House sentiment were against the Speaker. He therefore wrote a note to Reed, strongly urging him to permit the resolution to come up for consideration. Reed yielded and on June 15, 1898, the House approved the resolution by a vote of more than two to one. Reed was absent because of illness. To show the House and the country that he had not receded from his opposition, he requested the Speaker pro tem to have recorded that if he had been present he would have voted against the resolution.

The war with the Philippines which grew out of the war with Spain deepened the division between him and the Administration. He could not agree that the people of these islands should be forced to bow to control by the United States. Reed told his friend, Asher Hinds, "I have tried, perhaps not always successfully, to make the acts of my public life accord with my conscience, and I cannot now do this thing." He decided the time had come for him to retire from public life.

He resigned his House seat on September 4, 1899, and became affiliated with a New York law firm. He died in Washington, where he had gone on business, on December 7, 1902.

4

"Whoever at any time, whether for purposes of censure or rebuke or any other motive, attempts to lower the prestige of that office [Speaker of the House] by just so much lowers the prestige of the House itself, whose servant and exponent the Speaker is. No attack, whether open or covert, can be made upon that office without leaving to the future a legacy of disorder and bad government. This is not because the Speaker is himself a sacred creation. It is because he is the embodiment of the House, its power and dignity."

Thomas Reed, whose words those are, would have gagged at the thought of publicly linking himself with "the little people." He nevertheless had a strong feeling for the House of Representatives as the governmental institution closest to the American people. Any infringement on the "power and dignity" of the House was thus an insult to the people and to be resented and resisted as such. Similarly, any attack upon the speakership —again as an institution—was an attack against the whole House and against the whole people.

"Ultimately, the people govern," Reed said. "There are ostentatious actors here and there who stud the stage with panoply or with clanging arms, who seem to do many things; but in the end the popular feeling has its way." He was a strong partisan precisely because of his conviction that in a republic popular sentiment could be expressed effectively only through political organizations. "The moment you get a nonpartisan republic that republic is tottering to its fall," he said, and he believed it.

It was as a party leader who stood high above his associates that Reed won his position of authority. He could not be adjudged a great legislator. He did not become an expert on any of the issues that stirred the country during the twenty-two years that he served in Congress. He made few formal speeches, and when he did speak his oratory was not of a kind to sway the emotions of his audience. He was not a man who became carried away by "causes." He observed realistically that "one, with God, is always a majority, but many a martyr has been burned at the stake while the votes were being counted." He once ironically congratulated Theodore Roosevelt on his "original discovery of the Ten Commandments." He had strong convictions of his own on political philosophy and public policy. He pressed those convictions aggressively, but he held that evolution alone would remedy most existing evils in the nation's economic and social structure. He saw little need for government action to speed the evolutionary process.

Yet, in spite of any negative qualities, Reed was outstanding as a Speaker and as a human being.

He brought order to the House at a time when disorder threatened to stop the government from functioning. He set down a pattern for the speakership that, even after subsequent modifications, changed the nature of that office for all time. His party controlled the House only eight of the twenty-two years he was in Congress. For six of those eight years he occupied the Speaker's chair. His power came not alone from the rules he had caused the House to adopt but also from the force of his personality and from his intellectual prowess. The new system would work under the direction of other Speakers, but never as well as it worked under him. That, in fact, was its weakness. A Tom Reed was required to administer the Reed Rules.

Reed's absolute honesty, with himself and with others, was never questioned. He was by instinct and philosophy on the side of the business interests of his day, but there was never a suspicion that he profited personally by his support of measures that benefitted them. His attitude toward such interests was standoffish. For example, he would not use the privilege given to members of Congress of sending free telegrams from the Capitol. He explained, "The time may come when I shall want to hit one of these telegraph companies a wallop, and I don't want to put myself in a position where I shall be charged with ingratitude." Thomas Laffan of the New York *Sun*, his friend for many years, wrote after Reed's death, "The man was the soul of honesty. He was a statesman in spite of himself."

Although he had a cheerful disdain for the professional charms of a handshaking politician, Reed was known both by his few close friends and his casual companions as delightful company. This side of him was largely obscured from public view by his political activities and the controversy they engendered, for his natural humor seemed to come through most often as biting sarcasm. Among his intimates he was a different man. Henry Cabot Lodge thought that "no more agreeable companion ever lived," adding: "With the friends he cared for, and he was himself the most loyal of friends, he would sit or walk by the hour, talking of everything. The talk was always fresh, keen, and suggestive, and the great, hearty, contagious laugh would come at intervals and carry everyone with it."

Reed was the delight of newspaper reporters. A writing man of sorts himself, he understood their professional appetite for quotable quotes and was inclined to be cooperative even in answering questions that he regarded as nonsensical. A reporter, sent by his editor to get a "reaction story" (which consists, now as then, of statements of opinion by prominent persons on some event of current interest), asked the Speaker what he thought of a Papal message. Reed replied, "The overpowering unimportance of this makes me speechless. I have nothing to say." Another editor had the idea of getting together a symposium on "the greatest problem now confronting the American people." His reporter buttonholed Reed and put the question to the Speaker as he was walking toward the Capitol one morning. "How to dodge a bicycle," Reed drawled, ambling on his way.

He responded at greater length to a newsman who asked what he thought of resolutions passed by a post of the Grand Army of the Republic that took the Speaker to task for his refusal to aid in passing veterans' pension legislation. Reed observed that he attached little importance to the resolutions, since he had noted that every veterans' organization was likely to have among its membership a less desirable element. Such members get together, he went on, "and resolve three things. First, we saved the country; second, the country wouldn't have been saved if it hadn't been for us; third, we want it."

Reed could laugh at himself, even at his own autocratic pretensions. When a Southern Representative, one day putting his feet up on his desk, displayed an unusual stretch of white sock above each shoe, the Speaker sent an assistant sergeant of arms with the message: "The Czar commands you to haul down those flags of truce." And after viewing a portrait John Singer Sargent had done of him, Reed remarked painedly, "Well, I hope my enemies are satisfied now."

It can be dangerous for a man in public life to acquire a reputation as a humorist. Not to be taken seriously in politics is disastrous. Reed was never so threatened. He used humor as a weapon, and it was only one of many that he brought forth in debate in the House or in presiding over that body's deliberations. Despite his gaiety with friends and his mirth-rousing repartee in public, no one who knew Reed could fail to realize his great seriousness in his devotion to his duty and to his country.

He was a hard fighter for the tenets in which he believed. Yet, contradictorily, he had many qualities of what the French call *l'homme désengagé*. He frequently gave the impression of being a detached observer at the same time that he was an active participant, of being somewhat above the battle at the very moment that he was the leader of the forces against the opposition. "It is a very lonely life that a man leads," he said in a public address after his retirement from Congress, "who becomes aware of truths before their time." The somberness of that remark is as typical of Thomas Reed as any of his witticisms.

IV

Uncle Joe

JOSEPH GURNEY CANNON of Danville, Illinois, was sixty-seven
years old when he became Speaker of the United States House
of Representatives, and he was not a man afflicted with self-
doubt. He was ready, and more than ready, to take on the job.

Cannon had been a candidate for the speakership in 1889,
but ran a poor third to Thomas Reed. Although he dutifully
congratulated the victor and worked with him as a loyal and
anxious lieutenant, he afterward confessed that he was "vain
enough to believe that I was as good a man as Reed" and "the
speakership was my ambition." After Reed's retirement, Cannon, whatever his expectations, was again passed over. General David B. Henderson of Iowa, a one-legged hero of the
Civil War, was named Speaker, and Cannon had to wait
four more years, for Henderson was re-elected Speaker in the
Fifty-seventh Congress. Now, with the convening of the Fifty-
eighth in special session on November 9, 1903, Joseph G. Cannon's day had come.

The new Speaker was a hard-shell Republican in an era
when the Grand Old Party had become accustomed to working its will on the country. Party regularity was even more
meaningful to Cannon than the Methodism he, the son of
Quakers, had embraced after marrying a pretty Methodist
schoolteacher. He despised and did not profess to understand
Democrats and free traders. He was instinctively opposed to

all professional agitators, and was a tough, determined, and tireless fighter for his beliefs. Having had some part in formulating the Reed Rules for the governing of the House, having actively supported Reed in their application, he naturally believed very strongly in that code. He was against changing the rules or, indeed, anything else.

1

In many ways, Cannon was an almost perfect product of his time, circumstances, and physical surroundings. Although he had not served in the Civil War, he was outwardly the prototype of the garrulous old veterans known to every boy who loitered in the courthouse square of any small American town in the early years of the twentieth century. He liked to tell and listen to tall tales, enjoyed a robust joke, and thought stoutly of himself as a member of that unreal mass known then as "the common people" of the United States. "I am one of the great army of mediocrity which constitutes the majority," he said, and it was a boast. Gregarious by nature as well as by profession, he liked best of all the company of his political cronies and was immensely popular on both sides of the House. He was "Uncle Joe" to everyone.

He had been raised in the pioneer tradition that every man is as good as any other man and that the ideal American is one who can look any other man in the eye and tell him to go to hell. He had grown up in and had been shaped by the frontier West. Yet, during his long service in Congress, Cannon's interests were those of the moneyed and, to the folks of Danville, Illinois, the effete East. This attitude was not adopted or held in the hope that he would profit personally from serving the legislative interests of the corporations. It was simply that he believed as all the other solid people believed.

Although he was of the West, Joe Cannon was born in the South, in the hill country of North Carolina, on May 7, 1836. His father was a country doctor. In the early forties, the Cannon family joined the westward migration of the numerous Quaker colonies of the Carolinas. The Quakers had come into the South years earlier to escape the intolerance toward their religion they had suffered in New England. Now they left the South because of their abhorrence of slavery and their presentiment that armed conflict would come over the slavery issue. The North Carolina contingent, of which the Cannons were a part, went all the way to Illinois, stopping finally to build a new settlement in the timber belt along the Wabash River.

Young Joe's childhood and early youth were spent on a farm which the family, with plow and ax, cleared out of the forest. Home was a log cabin. When Joe was fourteen, his father was drowned while trying to cross a flooded creek on the way to visit a patient. The boy perforce became the head of the family. He went to work as a clerk in a country store at a salary of 150 dollars a year. After five years he could count his savings at five hundred dollars, and the family had managed to hold onto the farm. Although the youngster's education was of the meager kind obtainable in the country schools of the region, he took his savings and entered law school in Cincinnati, Ohio.

After six months in law school, he spent a year as a clerk in the office of a Terre Haute lawyer. Then, in 1858, when he was twenty-two years old he went to Shelbyville, Illinois, and opened his own law office. Clients did not besiege the young man. He moved on to Tuscola, county seat of the newly formed Coles County, still in Illinois, and hung out his shingle there. A year later he brought his mother and his brother, William, to Tuscola. In 1876 he moved to Danville and lived there— and in Washington—for the rest of his life.

Meanwhile, in 1862, he married Mary Reed, a Methodist schoolteacher. They had two daughters, one of whom, after Mrs. Cannon died in 1899, became Speaker Cannon's official hostess in Washington.

Meanwhile, also, the young lawyer had gone into politics.

He was defeated in his first effort, in 1860, to become district attorney of Coles County. But the following year he was elected to that post for a new district created by the Republican legislature. He occupied the office until 1872 when he was elected to his first term in the House of Representatives.

That was the year Ulysses S. Grant was elected to a second term as President. "It was a great year," Joseph Cannon recollected in 1922, in an interview with the New York *Times*. "It was the year when Vesuvius produced one of her worst and most historic eruptions. It was the year of the great Boston fire that burned up something like eighty million dollars' worth of property, the year they arrested Brigham Young and charged him with complicity in the murder of Richard Yates, the year when the Prohibitionists held their first national convention and nominated James Black of Pennsylvania for President, the year that Spain emancipated the slaves in Puerto Rico, and the year when Germany became an empire and France a republic."

In the United States, the new member of Congress dourly noted, it was also "a reform year, the beginning of a decade of 'reform' which shook up the virtues as well as the vices of the people. Nothing was right and nobody was safe from the reformers."

The gentleman from Illinois was prepared to fight the reformers all the way, both because of his own convictions and because he was confident that his anti-reform, high-tariff, keep-things-as-they-are stand accurately reflected the majority sentiment of the Illinois district he had been chosen to represent.

In the year that Cannon took his seat, Chief Justice Edward G. Ryan of the Wisconsin Supreme Court, addressing students at the University of Wisconsin, said: "There is looming up a new and dark power. The accumulation of individual wealth seems to be greater than it ever has been since the downfall of the Roman Empire. The enterprises of the country are aggregating vast corporate combinations of unexampled capital, boldly marching not for economic conquests only, but for political power. For the first time really in our politics, money is taking the field as an organized power."

If Cannon had known of Ryan's speech, he no doubt would have wondered what the judge was complaining about.

James G. Blaine was Speaker of the House. From him Cannon requested and received an appointment to the Committee on Post Offices and Post Roads. He wanted the assignment because it would help him to carry out a plan that he knew would be popular in the rural district he represented. At that time newspapers and magazines were mailed without prepayment of postage. Each of some thirty-three thousand postmasters in the country had the responsibility of collecting postage from the individual subscribers. Cannon introduced a bill providing that the publications should be weighed at the office of mailing and the postage prepaid by the publishers. Although the publishers generally opposed this proposal to transfer the postage cost to them from their subscribers, Cannon's bill was passed by both House and Senate, and he was proud of it all his life.

Cannon's maiden speech in the House was made in defense of this bill and a companion proposal to permit all public documents, including seeds for farm or garden use, to be sent postage-free by members of Congress to their constituents. The House had its first sample of the Cannon oratorical style. He was far from a polished speaker, but the slender blond man with the flaxen chin whiskers attracted immediate attention by his earnestness and his forthright, hoarsely shouted use of homely language. His gestures were spectacular. As he warmed to his subject, his arms flailed the air like windmill blades, his left fist repeatedly whacked the palm of his right hand, and the long tails of his unbuttoned coat fluttered out behind him. His speeches were physical combats.

In defending the free mailing of seed by congressmen, Cannon made himself so much at one with the farmers of his district that a New Jersey member, Walter William Phelps, broke in to say dryly, "The gentleman from Illinois must have oats in his pocket."

"Yes!" cried Cannon. "I have oats in my pocket and hay-seed in my hair, and the Western people generally are affected the same way. And we expect that the seed, being good, will yield a good crop."

House members laughed and applauded their new colleague. And, said Phelps a few days later, "that hayseed glowed around his head like a halo."

One effect of this exchange was that, combined with his rather startling appearance in debate, it brought Cannon early notice from the Washington correspondents of out-of-town newspapers. From then on, when news was scarce, the corre-spondents were apt to write an off-beat story about the member from the Danville, Illinois, district. He complained that the reporters always wrote of him as a "character" instead of giving sober attention to his political principles and legislative activi-ties. He thought they did not take him seriously enough.

He engaged frequently in floor debate in the years before he became Speaker. He was at his best when defending a bill for which he had responsibility. As a district attorney riding the court circuit in Illinois he had of necessity become an expert in rough and ready argument. He used the same method in the House. He disdained prepared speeches and depended on his knowledge of the subject at hand to see him through. He was never to be led off into side arguments that had nothing to do with the issue under consideration. At the same time, he was shrewd, even cunning, in diverting his opponents off the main track. He drew attention to his own arguments partly because, while speaking, he was constantly in motion. Champ Clark of Missouri called him "The Dancing Dervish of Illinois." Speaker Reed once interrupted him to drawl, "Joe, are you making this speech on mileage?"

Cannon was not merely a talker. He was a worker too. As a member of the Post Office Committee, he devoted himself to becoming an authority on postal matters. Later, as he advanced up the House ladder and became chairman of the Appropria-tions Committee, he applied himself with equal assiduity to learn all he could about government fiscal matters—especially how to keep down expenditures. All the while, too, he was making friends among Republicans and Democrats alike. Few could hold themselves aloof from his genial good-fellowship.

In an intensely partisan period, Cannon's unswerving party loyalty was noted by the House leadership. To him, as Brand Whitlock said of the Midwest as a whole, Republicanism was "a fundamental and self-evident thing like life, liberty, and the pursuit of happiness, or the flag or the federal judiciary." He unquestioningly walked the party path. For example, he led an attack in a caucus of House Republicans against an 1890 bill which proposed to set up a system of strict control of Federal elections in the South. Despite his opposition, the caucus approved the bill by one vote, making it a party measure. Partyman Cannon, by this time a member of the Rules Committee, turned around and brought from that committee an order for immediate consideration of the bill, then drove it through the House with virtually unanimous Republican support. The party regulars could count on Cannon any time, every time.

The fight over the adoption of Reed's rules, in which he was a vigorous participant, further improved his standing with his Republican colleagues. The rules themselves, by greatly strengthening the majority's power in the House, enhanced Cannon's position. And then, just as it appeared certain he was to go on to an even greater position, he was rejected by his constituents in the election of 1890, which was so catastrophic to Republicans generally.

Not long after the election, Cannon, in Chicago, met two other defeated members of the Sixty-first Congress, William McKinley of Ohio and Senator Thomas Carter of Montana. These two belittled their defeat. Carter remarked that it suited him just as well to get out of Congress; McKinley claimed he was glad things had turned out as they had.

Cannon would have none of that. "That's what I'm saying to everyone else," he told them, "but, boys, don't let's lie to one another. It hurts, and it hurts damned bad."

He did not lie to himself, and he was determined to regain his seat in the House. That was his only chance to wade in the national political puddle, for the Illinois legislature twice refused to send him to the United States Senate. He was a candidate again for the House in 1892, and this time he won. He returned to loyal service to the Republican leadership, and in 1903, thirty years after he had first entered Congress, he received the reward he felt he had completely earned.

He was Speaker.

2

Theodore Roosevelt, who was in the White House, wasted no time in making it clear that he would work closely with the new Speaker. This was the period in which Roosevelt thought that he wanted to, and that he could, get along amicably with the business interests. The earlier talk about Roosevelt being unsafe for the country had largely died out. Business had decided, Cannon said, that Roosevelt's bark was worse than his bite, "although often his bark was annoying enough."

In any case, no politically knowledgeable observer doubted that the Rough Rider would be nominated for his own term at the 1904 Republican convention. The President was taking no chances, however, so he consulted frequently with Cannon to keep in touch with the sentiments of House Republicans. In fact, he courted the Speaker with all his charm. When Cannon declined an invitation to a White House dinner because he was to be seated below the Attorney General and considered it a slight to the House of Representatives, Roosevelt proceeded to give a dinner with the Speaker himself as guest of honor. Presidents have been following Theodore Roosevelt's example ever since.

The two men consulted several times a week, sometimes daily, when Congress was in session. In the first-person book, a sort of autobiography, written for him by his long-time secretary, L. White Busbey, Cannon made it clear that his frequent calls at the White House were made at the President's request. When there were newspaper reports of hard feeling between them, Roosevelt wrote a note to the Speaker to say, "I care not a rap about the reports of clashes and the predictions of clashes between you and me. We can handle the matter ourselves. Come up some evening for a long talk . . . and let me know when to expect you."

Their backgrounds being so totally different, there inevitably were many differences in outlook. Roosevelt was, for all time, Oyster Bay, New York; Cannon was, no less uncompromisingly, country Illinois. Not even political necessities could keep them always in harmony. Cannon once exasperatedly told a friend, "That fellow at the other end of the Avenue wants everything from the birth of Christ to the death of the devil." When they disagreed, the Speaker held his own. Roosevelt did not overtly push him around. He told an adviser who suggested that the President should "lay down on Uncle Joe" that he felt it would be "a good deal like laying down on a hedgehog." Cannon, on his part, recognized the President as leader of the Republican Party—indeed, he remarked, "I don't think it would be an exaggeration to say that he was the party's dictator."

The Speaker had reason, on the whole, to feel satisfied. He was in the position he had long coveted; he was listened to with care by the President, liked by most of his colleagues, and respected by all of them. Tariff rates were high, and the outlook was rosy from the vantage point of the Speaker's Room in the Capitol. If there were rumblings over the country, they did not reach him. And if they had reached him he would have known without even thinking about the matter that they came from free traders and Democrats. Everybody knew what was to be expected of that lot.

Mark Sullivan, in his journalistic history of the first quarter of the twentieth century, wrote:

"There was in America, during the years preceding 1900 and for many years thereafter, a prevailing mood. It was a mood of irritation. The average American in great numbers had the feeling that he was being 'put upon' by something he couldn't quite see or get his fingers on; that someone was 'riding' him; that some force or other was 'crowding' him. Vaguely he felt that his freedom of action, his opportunity to do as he pleased, was being frustrated in ways mysterious in their origin and operation, and in their effects most uncomfortable; that his economic freedom as well as his freedom of action, and his capacity to direct his political liberty toward the results he desired, was being circumscribed in a tightening ring, the drawing-strings of which, he felt sure, were being pulled by the hands of some invisible power which he ardently desired to see and get at, but could not. This unseen enemy he tried to personify. He called it the Invisible Government, the Money Interests, the Gold Bug, Wall Street, the Trusts. During the first Bryan campaign, the spokesman of the West spoke of the business men of the East, collectively, as 'the enemy.' "

Speaker Joseph G. Cannon did not in any way share this "prevailing mood." Everything was all right. The country had prospered for forty years under a protective tariff, he explained in a 1904 campaign speech, and 92 per cent of the country's markets had been developed at home. Free traders were motivated by either "prejudice or crankiness." As for labor, its demands were simply ridiculous. Presented with a "bill of grievances" by Samuel Gompers, president of the American Federation of Labor, Cannon lashed out at the labor leader: "You are not the whole shooting match. You are not the only pebble on the beach." Heckled by suffragettes, he offered the opinion that women did not really want to vote and, anyway, he twinkled, no person was entitled to more than one vote and a woman would have her own and her husband's. To conservationists seeking a modest appropriation for a project they favored, the Speaker snapped, "Not one damned cent for scenery!"

He ran the House of Representatives as it had never been run before. The deadly rapier wielded by Reed gave way to a bludgeon, which at first he used only to knock down Democrats. Lacking Reed's urbanity, Cannon also was without the former Speaker's glacial coldness. He had a warm feeling for his fellowman, a feeling that was intensified if the fellowman was a member of the House—and especially if he was a Republican.

People who knew Cannon liked him—that was it. They liked his rough humor, his studied unconventionality, his heavy pretense of being a hayseed, and his sentimentality, and they liked the spirit of youthfulness that emanated from him even as he approached his seventieth year. The chin whiskers had turned white and the hairline had receded from his forehead, but the blue-gray eyes sparkled zestfully, the body was still lean and erect, the cheeks still ruddy. A cigar was his trade mark. He kept one thrust into the left side of his mouth during most of his waking hours, while from the right side poured an unending stream of anecdotes, reminiscences, political conversation, and mild profanity.

A female reporter for the New York *World,* who wrote under the pseudonym of Kate Carew, came down to Washington in 1904 to interview the Speaker, and was fascinated. She found him to be (in only part of a champion nonstop sentence) "a very punctilious and debonair gentleman of middle age, with a great deal of natural dignity, very vital, very much in love with the world and sunshine and people; gallant, gay, with graceful social gifts and a store of old-fashioned chivalry, keen, clean, American, masculine, and, though renowned for his humor, not a bit more remarkable for that quality than for a deep and strong fibre of sentiment, which I make bold to proclaim the most essential of his attributes."

Although less inclined than this lady to gushiness, nearly all the members of the House were genuinely fond of the modest and essentially kindly man in the Speaker's chair. Reed had ruled the House virtually alone. Cannon had friends all around him. A contemporary writer, George Fitch, in *American Magazine,* described him as a man who "loves to raise the tariff in the afternoon and raise the ante in the evening with a pleasant little semi-occasional game between friends." The pleasantness of the off-duty sessions had much to do with Cannon's effectiveness in on-duty sessions. A great deal of House business was transacted at the private get-togethers over a few drinks and between poker hands.

And, of course, he always had the Reed Rules to back him when necessary.

He also had on his side the binding party caucus which the Republicans utilized as a weapon in enforcing party discipline. When two-thirds of the House Republicans reached a decision on any legislative proposal, that was it. Would-be dissidents had to go along if they valued their political future. Cannon could use, and did use, the caucus to enable his party to present before the nation a surface aspect of unanimous agreement on national issues.

"An able man and a clever politician in the Chair owns the House of Representatives body, soul, and conscience," wrote Hubert Bruce Fuller, and the description of Cannon was perfect. The Speaker summed it up when he told John Sharp Williams of Mississippi, House leader for the Democrats, "I am going to be as fair as I can, consistent with the exigencies of American politics."

He and Williams, one as partisan as the other, were warm personal friends. Just prior to the adjournment of the Fifty-eighth Congress, Williams paid a glowing tribute to the Speaker "in recognition of kindly services and kindly feeling already extended and already appreciated." Another Democrat, Champ Clark, was likewise impressed by the "extraordinary kindness" prevailing among members of that Congress.

The kindness, however real, was strictly personal. It did not extend to politics either in that Congress or in any other when Cannon was Speaker. He had repeatedly proclaimed his belief in "a government by and of parties." His party held a majority in the House and his leadership was, as a matter of course, to be exercised for the benefit of the majority. Asked by a member if there was a possibility that a certain bill could be passed, Cannon ruled from the Chair, "This House could pass an elephant if the gentleman in charge of it could catch the Speaker's eye." A slight grin creasing his face, he closed his eyes and called for the next order of business. After a voice vote on another bill, he pounded his gavel and cried, "The ayes make the most noise, but the nays have it."

The fact was that, not content with Reed's rules, he created his own rules as he went along. On a motion made by a Democrat, who knew it would fail but who wanted to get the majority on record, a rising vote was demanded. Five or six Democrats rose in the affirmative, followed by half the membership of the House standing in the negative. Cannon began to count. "One, two, three," he counted, "four——oh, hell, a hundred!" The vote was recorded that way. When a freshman member from Tennessee, a Democrat named Cordell Hull, wanted to offer an income tax amendment to a tariff bill, the Speaker simply ignored him.

Small wonder that when a constituent asked one sardonic Representative to send him a copy of the House rules he received a photograph of Speaker Cannon.

A steady drumbeat of editorial opposition came from the press to call attention to the Speaker's highhandedness. The cartoons in Democratic papers caricatured "Uncle Joe" Cannon more savagely than they ever had "Czar" Reed. Visitors to the House gallery were interested, first of all, in seeing Cannon, although they rarely knew what to expect. A woman visitor once expressed amazement as the Speaker stood and bowed his head with the other members during the chaplain's opening prayer. "There's old Joe Cannon," she whispered to a friend, "an' him a-prayin'. The old hypocrite!"

There was no visible limit to the Speaker's exercise of personal authority. Although he often proclaimed his wholehearted adherence to the principle of majority rule, in practice he hardly bothered to carry on the fiction that the House relied on the Republican majority to set its course.

During each session he would state on his own what legislation would be enacted and what bills would fail to pass. On the rare occasions that he took any notice of criticism, Cannon made the technical defense that the members could change everything at any time they chose. They could take the speakership away from him. They could revise the rules. They had the power, by majority vote, to exercise absolute control over all legislation. Committees, not the Speaker, had the power to keep bills bottled up or to report them to the House for action. And so on.

Although he offered this defense with a straight face, Cannon knew well enough that any Republican member would be slow—would deem it foolish—to defy the wishes of the man who handed out committee assignments, who had complete freedom of choice as to whether he should extend or withhold recognition on the floor, and who could advance or kill any Representative's pet legislative project.

Furthermore, it was the Speaker who named the committee chairmen. The House at that time had sixty-two standing committees, and the chairmanship of even the most innocuous was a prize eagerly sought. And reasonably enough. Before the first House Office Building became available to members in 1908, committee chairmen were the only Representatives to whom private offices were assigned. Moreover, a chairman received free stationery and was paid an extra 125 dollars a month to employ a clerk. And the committee chairman was extended special privileges—at, naturally, the discretion of the Speaker—in House procedure. A committee chairman had a better chance, to deal in understatement, of having a bill passed than an ordinary member.

All in all, defiance of the Speaker by one of his own party was highly improbable.

As for the Democratic members, they were hardly worth thinking about—except, of course, as good fellows personally. They were the minority, and this was a country, this was a House, where the majority ruled. Williams, the ranking Democrat on the Rules Committee, explained the Democrats' plight when he set forth his own: "I am invited to the seances, but I am never consulted about the spiritualistic appearances."

Still, in spite of everything, the House loved its Speaker. On Capitol Hill, Cannon was regarded as having freed the House from domination by the Senate. He was known for his determination not to give way to Senate members of the conference committees to which legislation was sent for reconciling differences between the versions passed by the two bodies. In this and other ways, Cannon made it mean something to be a member of the House.

The President also tried to love him. At the White House, statements praising the Speaker came frequently from Roosevelt as he finished out the term to which McKinley had been elected and then started his own full term of office. Thus, in 1906, the President was saying publicly that he had no "stouter friend" than Cannon. "He is a patriotic American," Roosevelt declared. "He is for every man, rich or poor, capitalist or labor man, so long as he is a decent American, and he is entitled to our support because he is a patriotic man."

Cannon read that statement with pleasure, but he did not see what the President wrote his friend, Henry Cabot Lodge, only a few weeks later: "Cannon came to New York, where he made a two and a quarter hours' speech on the tariff, the history of the Republican party, the full dinner pail, and various other topics about which the people in New York this year are no more concerned than they were with the embargo or the Dred Scott decision." The meeting, in Roosevelt's opinion, was a "fizzle."

Yet, during the same 1906 congressional campaign, the consummate politician in the White House wrote to Cannon's friend and the Republican party whip in the House, James E. Watson of Indiana: "With Mr. Cannon as Speaker, working hand in hand and in hearty fashion with the Senate, Congress has accomplished a literally phenomenal amount of work. It has shown courage, good sense, and patriotism that it would be a real and serious misfortune for the country to fail to recognize."

After the election was over, however, it became evident that the strain of the enforced cordiality between the two strong-minded men was beginning to tell. The muckrakers of the era were getting under Roosevelt's skin with their exposés of trusts and big-business practices in general. The "common people" were becoming increasingly antagonistic toward the giant corporations. Roosevelt, not planning to run for re-election in 1908, was less concerned than he had been earlier about whether his policies pleased business. He saw a social crisis at hand and thought the government had to move to meet it. Not so Speaker Cannon. To him, America was "a great success from every standpoint," and he could perceive "very little unrest" among the people. Admittedly, "a few demagogues" were at work to discredit the American system. "But," said Cannon, "the people are too busy, too prosperous, to make calamity-howling a success."

One specific point of difference had to do with the President's support of efforts to get pure food and meat inspection laws enacted by Congress. Upton Sinclair had written a book called *The Jungle*, in which he painted a lurid picture of both working and sanitary conditions in the huge meat packing plants of Chicago. The book caused a great public outcry, mainly from people whose digestive sensibilities were affronted, but the powerful man in the Speaker's chair had only to look back to his own boyhood to know that the need for the proposed legislation was greatly exaggerated. "We had no trouble about pure food laws or canned goods," he recalled, "for the meat came from the hog pen or the pasture where the cattle and sheep grew fat, the butter came from the family churn, and the canned berries were homemade."

Roosevelt, both for public consumption and in his personal contacts with Cannon, continued for a time to pretend that all was well between the two. He flatteringly wrote Cannon that "my experience has been that your judgment is rather more apt to be sound than mine in such matters [of domestic legislation]," and pleaded, "Now, Uncle Joe, stand by me if you can."

But how could the apostle of things as they were stand by

a President who proposed such heresies as an income tax and an inheritance tax, Federal licensing of corporations, Federal investigation of labor disputes, laws to govern the employment of women and children, letting newsprint and wood pulp enter the country free of duty, and Federal supervision of railroad securities?

Of the tax proposals, Cannon said stiffly, "In my judgment, it is not wise to increase the revenue of the Government nor is it necessary or advisable to transfer burdens from the local and state treasuries to the Federal Treasury to foster a centralizing power and responsibility which of necessity develops fast enough." Nor was he more indulgently disposed toward the other radical proposals that had come from the White House.

To Cannon and others it looked as if Mark Hanna had been right, after all, in opposing the vice-presidential nomination that placed "the damned cowboy" in succession for the presidency. The Democratic party might be, as a New York *Sun* editorial said, "permanently and dangerously impulsive," but there was more and more thinking among old-line Republicans that the same could be accurately said about the Republican President.

Cannon liked the story about Roosevelt told by John Morley, the English politician and historian. After a visit to the United States, Morley was asked by a woman at a London dinner party what he thought of Roosevelt. He began a pontifical reply: "You may take every adjective on every page of the *Oxford Dictionary*, good, bad, indifferent, and you will find someone to apply it——"

"That's too complicated," his questioner interrupted impatiently. "Can't you tell us in half a dozen words?"

"In half a dozen words," Morley responded, "half St. Paul, half St. Vitus."

"Half St. Paul, half St. Vitus!" Cannon would repeat, barking with laughter as he told the story.

A cartoon in *Harper's Weekly* showed the President and the Speaker grappling for control of the steering wheel of an automobile labeled G.O.P., while a worried Uncle Sam looked on from the back seat. The Washington *Post* suggested that Roosevelt had plans to get a new Speaker who would be more in accord with his policies. But if the President had such a goal in mind, he realistically never declared himself on it openly. In any case, Cannon's constituents continued to send him back to Congress, and his Republican colleagues continued to elect him Speaker of the House.

Nevertheless, as the presidential election year of 1908 approached, storm warnings were becoming clearly visible on the political horizon.

Like many another House Speaker, Cannon had vague presidential aspirations of his own. As far back as 1905, his colleagues had been telling him that he had as good a chance for the nomination as anyone else. His secretary believed Cannon did not consider himself "intellectually unfit" to be President. Lincoln, he could tell himself, had come from a background much like his. When he was a young man, he had even met Lincoln two or three times, and he rather fancied there were certain resemblances between them. As for the politics of the matter, he was confident he could gain the support of most of the 222 Republican members of the House. So went the dreams of the seventy-two-year-old politician.

But Roosevelt wanted William Howard Taft as his successor, and at the convention Taft was nominated on the first ballot. The convention was not, however, without its satisfactions for Cannon. He strongly influenced the platform and was instrumental in the choice of James S. Sherman of New York, one of his staunchest henchmen in the House, for Vice-President. "Sunny Jim" Sherman was not on the list of men Taft considered acceptable as a running mate. But, for all that, Sherman also was nominated on the first ballot for Vice-President after a seconding speech by Cannon brought resounding applause from the delegates.

The old man was at his best with the party regulars who attended national conventions. The understanding between them was complete.

However, if he was a hero to the delegates, he was not to the country. During the campaign there was an increasing flood of denunciation of him by the press as an unconscionable tyrant, the dictator of the House of Representatives, the repressive foe of every new legislative idea that had been put forward during the past third of a century. Newspaper cartoons pictured him as The Unrepentant Defendant in the court trial of Predatory Wealth for its victimizing of The Common People.

Cannon attributed the newspaper opposition to his refusal to support Roosevelt's proposal to permit the duty-free importation of newsprint and wood pulp. Besides, he contended, the publishers had never forgiven him for his long-ago bill requiring them to pay the cost of mailing their wares. Not for a moment did he concede that the progressivism he scorned had behind it any significant degree of popular sentiment.

The Democrats seized on Cannon and Cannonism as one of their principal campaign issues. Thundered their platform: "The House of Representatives, as controlled in recent years by the Republican party, has ceased to be a deliberative and legislative body, responsive to the will of a majority of its members, but has come under the absolute domination of the Speaker, who has entire control of its deliberations and powers of legislation. . . . Legislative government becomes a failure when one member, in the person of the Speaker, is more powerful than the entire body." William Jennings Bryan, in accepting the Democratic nomination, declared the overwhelming issue to be whether the people should rule. "They cannot do so," he said, "unless they can control the House of Representatives." But the House, he pointed out, was controlled by one man.

An all-out effort was mounted to bring about Cannon's defeat in his home district in Illinois and so make moot the question of whether he would continue as Speaker.

Bryan himself went into the Danville area to campaign against Cannon. The Speaker in return sneered at "The Commoner" as a "poor man's candidate" who had made a million dollars selling "wind and ink" on the Chautauqua circuit. Gompers traveled to Illinois to express labor's viewpoint: "It is quite evident that Cannon controls the banks, the business, and the booze of Danville. . . . If you love him so much, you will do the American people a great service if you will keep him home with you." Cannon retorted sharply, "The offense that brings me under condemnation is that as a Republican in Congress and Speaker of the House, I have refused to take orders from him and to agree to a scheme of legislation which would make one law for one set of Americans and another law for all other citizens." The conservationists campaigned hard against Cannon. So did the more numerous and better organized prohibitionists.

The Republicans themselves wished this particular issue would go away. Taft wrote to a friendly editor, "Confidentially, the great weight I have to carry in this campaign is Cannonism." He added his hope that if the Republicans controlled the House in the next Congress they would elect a new Speaker. He also predicted to Roosevelt that the Republicans would have only a small majority in the House, "with enough men who will refuse to vote for Cannon to defeat him for Speaker." Roosevelt replied, "I feel just as you do about Cannon."

Taft's prediction was wrong. He had expected to get between 275 and 300 electoral votes, but his total was 321 to 162 for Bryan. In the House, the Republicans lined up a healthy majority, taking 219 seats to 172 for the Democrats. Cannon himself won by ten thousand votes. And out in Nebraska, a young Republican Representative named George W. Norris, who had made slashing campaign attacks against Cannonism, squeaked through to re-election by only twenty-two votes out of more than forty thousand cast.

"The people do rule," Cannon wired the President-elect, undoubtedly chuckling in his whiskers.

His opponents had chosen to make Cannonism a national issue. They had lost and he had won. The leaders of his own party, Taft and Roosevelt, ruefully concluded that Cannon could not be defeated for re-election as Speaker. They were right. The House met in special session March 15, 1909, and

Cannon received 204 votes for Speaker to 166 for Champ Clark. Four other members received a total of twelve votes, representing the number of House Republicans daring enough to put themselves on record against "Uncle Joe."

But the storm clouds that hovered around the Speaker's head refused to go away.

During Cannon's earlier years in the Chair only scattered mutterings had been heard about his strenuous application of the Reed Rules. The trouble was that the longer he stayed in power, the more power he abrogated to himself. Members must see him in advance of seeking recognition on the floor. Their plans had to be approved by him if they were to have any chance of obtaining recognition. He stacked the key committees with men who would unquestioningly support everything he favored and oppose everything he was against. He arbitrarily took chairmanships away from members who tried to flout his authority.

There was now a hard core of Insurgents, small in number but persistent in endeavor, on the Republican side of the House. Their complaints had been loud in the lame-duck session of the Sixtieth Congress, but despite the noise they had made they were able to muster only a dozen votes against Cannon in the Sixty-first Congress. Then, on the usual motion to adopt the House rules of the previous Congress, Champ Clark, the new Democratic floor leader, forced a roll-call vote. The rules momentarily were not readopted, but Clark lost on a resolution that would have established a Rules Committee of fifteen members—six Democrats, five regular Republicans, and four Insurgents. Finally, an amendment was adopted making certain changes in the rules, including a provision for a unanimous consent calendar. This would relieve the members of the necessity of going to the Speaker, "hat in hand," to get his permission to take up private and uncontested bills.

It was not much of a victory for the Insurgents, but Cannon took note of it when he announced the composition of the committees. Three Insurgents were removed from committee chairmanships. Others were taken off the major committees and put on the lesser committees.

The Speaker paid his respects to the rebels in characteristic terms: "Adam and Eve were insurgents and ate of the forbidden fruit, expecting to become gods. They only learned to see their own nakedness. Judas was an insurgent and sold his Master for thirty pieces of silver. I have no doubt he would have been applauded by the newspapers in Jerusalem had there been any in that day."

Cannon's idea was that those Republicans who insisted on calling themselves Progressives should go all the way and openly join the Democrats. That would leave the Republican party in the hands of those to whom it had belonged for so many years.

The trouble was that Republicans, or many of them, were also changing. Some of the newer House members objected to a monolithic stand by the party on all national issues. Worst of all, among the most vociferous Insurgents were a few members from Cannon's own Midwest.

The Speaker, in facing his troubles, received neither aid nor encouragement from the new President. He really did not expect either, for he had but a small opinion of Taft as a party man. When Edward Douglass White, a Catholic and a Democrat, who had been appointed to the Supreme Court by President Grover Cleveland, was advanced to Chief Justice by Taft, Cannon was enraged. "The trouble with Taft," he sneered, "is that if he were Pope he would think it necessary to appoint a few Protestant Cardinals."

As for Taft, he at the same time detested Cannon and also feared his power. He had no experience in dealing with Congress. He thought he would get along better with Cannon out of the speakership—he had thought so even before his election—but he had no idea how such a happy event could be brought about.

Immediately after the election Taft had told an adviser, "I cannot take part in the movement to defeat Mr. Cannon for Speaker, however much such a movement would accord with my wishes or with the welfare of the Republican party." Writing to another complainant about Cannon, he said petulantly, "The election of a Speaker of the House is not within my consent. I have no jurisdiction in respect to the matter." He wished he did have. In still another letter, written before the first regular session began in December, 1909, he lamented, "There is now only one feature of the situation that I look forward to with considerable concern, and that is the continuation in politics of Cannon." He added hopefully, "I think he has been sufficiently honored to justify him in now retiring and in announcing his retirement, at least from the speakership contest, in advance of the next general election."

Similar wishful thinking was engaged in by others than the President. Lodge told Roosevelt that the Republicans would certainly lose the House in 1910 unless there was assurance that Cannon would not again stand for Speaker. Some went so far as to hope he would not even try for re-election to Congress. Leading Republican newspapers editorially suggested that he step down and out.

Cannon had no patience with such foolish talk. "I will say positively," he growled, "that I will not retire from Congress until my constituents fail to give me a majority. My worst enemies have never accused me of cowardice, but if I retired under fire both my friends and my enemies would be justified in not only calling me a coward but a poltroon."

The growing storm of criticism did not cause him to turn meek or even mild. Addressing one public meeting, he belligerently pulled back the lapels of his coat and cried, "Behold Mr. Cannon, the Beelzebub of Congress! Gaze on this noble manly form—me, Beelzbub! Me, the Czar!"

The Insurgents waited and planned.

3

A few years earlier, Blaine had described those bolters from the Republican party, the Mugwumps, as being "noisy but not numerous; pharisaical but not practical; ambitious but not wise; pretentious but not powerful." Cannon, with a few scurrilous and sometimes blasphemous additions of his own, had a like disregard for the Insurgents. Some, he conceded, were honest, if misguided, and "really believed they were victims of the Speaker." They were the exceptions. More of them were "dishonest and disgruntled and loaded their failures on the Speaker." They introduced demagogic bills which they knew would never be approved by the House and then told the "ignorant element" among their constituents that the measures would have been passed except for Cannon's personal opposition, "thus creating the belief that the Speaker was a 'Czar' and controlled by the 'interests.' "

Cannon's intelligence system in the House was excellent. He knew who the Insurgents were and what they were up to. He was keenly, although not fearfully, aware that ten or twelve Republican members were coming together almost nightly to lay plans—"plotting" was the word the Speaker used—to take away his power.

The unruly group included Victor Murdock, a sharp-tongued, redheaded Representative from Kansas, known for his often reiterated statement that if the Federal Constitution had provided that Congress should consist of the Senate and the Speaker of the House, it would never have been ratified—Murdock, who defined Cannonism as being "founded in the belief that the popular desire is unsafe." Another incorrigible Insurgent was Henry Allen Cooper of Wisconsin, from whom, in Cannon's acidulous words, "insurgency oozed at every pore even when he was in a state of suspended animation, which was not often." Two other Wisconsin Representatives, Irvine L. Lenroot and John Nelson, were members of the group, along with Miles Poindexter of Washington and Asle J. Gronna of North Dakota. So were two Minnesotans, Charles A. Lindbergh, a chronic opponent of the status quo, and Charles R. Davis.

Then there was Norris—George W. Norris of Nebraska.

His leadership of the Insurgents was an especially sore point with the Speaker. When Norris first came to Congress in 1903, the very year that Cannon assumed the speakership, he had been generally considered a safe addition to the ranks of the regular Republicans. In his early forties and with a record of sound Republicanism behind him in Nebraska, Norris had shown no tendencies toward Insurgency during his first few years in Congress. Yet here he was, only a little while later, writing in *La Follette's Weekly,* that Bible of Insurgency: "So far as the enactment of legislation is concerned, the House of Representatives bears about the same relation to the national government as the appendix does to the human body. It has no well-recognized function. For all practical purposes our national government, like Gaul of old, is divided into three parts: the Senate, the President, and the Speaker. This perversion of the real intent and object of the Constitution has been brought about so gradually and quietly that until recently the people have not understood the method of its accomplishment."

That was bad enough, but the thoughtful, heavy-lidded Nebraskan did not content himself with combatting Cannonism with words.

He successfully defied the Speaker on the floor of the House when he was ruled out of order in an attempt to amend a tariff bill to reduce the tariff on petroleum to one per cent. Norris appealed to the House for fair play, and Cannon's decision was overturned by a smashing vote of 322 to 47. Again, after Taft had fired Gifford Pinchot as Chief United States Forester and a congressional investigation was ordered, Norris made a motion that the investigating committee be named by the whole House rather than by the Speaker. Pinchot had many friends in the House, and enough of them joined the Insurgents on this question to carry Norris' motion by a vote of 149 to 146. The Speaker was furious.

Cannon recognized Norris as a dangerous foe. While his confidence in the righteousness of his conduct never wavered for an instant, he was too much aware of the political realities to discount the Insurgents' strength when it was added to that of Champ Clark and his Democrats. The motives of the latter the Speaker could at least understand if not approve. Democratic opposition was all in the game, but resistance, even antagonism, from members who had been elected on the Republican ticket was medicine too bitter to swallow. The embattled Speaker grew increasingly testy during the early months of 1910.

The climactic struggle began with an abruptness that was seeming rather than real.

Norris for weeks had been carrying about in his coat pocket a resolution to reform the procedure for determining House rules. He and his night-school colleagues had prepared the resolution with care. Norris' problem was how to obtain recognition from the Speaker to introduce the resolution—it was exceedingly difficult for Cannon to "see" the Representative from Nebraska on the House floor.

That was the situation on March 16 when Edgar Crumpacker, chairman of the Commitee on the Census, called up, out of order, a joint resolution regarding the taking of the Census of 1910. Crumpacker argued that the Constitution provided for the census to be taken during the year and that a mandate of the Constitution overrode any rule of the House. Cannon ruled that his argument was valid. On an appeal, the majority voted not to sustain the ruling.

Cannon had felt "in my bones" that this would happen. "So," he commented bitterly, "in a House supposed to have a Republican majority, a Republican Speaker in a parliamentary sense was knocked down, kicked about, and his face rubbed in the sand." He was not accustomed to such treatment and did not care for it.

Crumpacker's resolution was passed the next day, although Cannon declined to make another ruling on whether it was constitutionally privileged, having decided, in his words, "to let the House determine the matter." As he said, he probably would have again been overruled by the House, because many members were in a mood to oppose whatever the Speaker did. Times had changed since Tom Reed had told a Representative that he would never live to see the House reject a ruling by the Speaker, and Joseph G. Cannon knew the change was not for the better.

Norris saw his opportunity. He got to his feet to announce that he wished—as Crumpacker had done—to offer a resolution made privileged by the Constitution. Told to state it, if it was indeed privileged, the Nebraskan officially proposed his resolution to create a new Rules Committee. This committee, holding life-or-death power over any proposed legislation, still consisted of five members appointed by the Speaker, who was ex officio chairman. Norris' resolution provided that the committee would be enlarged to fifteen members, all elected by the House. The Speaker would be ineligible for membership on the committee.

It was true, Norris admitted, choosing his words with care, that his resolution might seem to defy existing rules, it not having been considered by any committe or reported to the House. Since, however, a majority of the body had upheld Crumpacker's plea of constitutional privilege, he claimed the same privilege for his resolution. After all, he pointed out with deceptive mildness, the Constitution did provide that the House should determine its own rules of procedure.

The purpose of the resolution was plain, glaringly so to Cannon. It was designed to overthrow him. It would put control of the Rules Committee and thus of the business of the House in the hands of an unholy alliance of Democrats and Insurgent Republicans. This combination would represent, as he saw it, "not a majority of the electorate but two opposing minority functions." The Speaker would become simply the presiding officer, his power restricted to placing motions before the House and declaring the results of votes. This was revolutionary, Cannon cried, and worse—"it was the recognition of anarchy under the color of law."

The Speaker and his lieutenants had known about the Norris

resolution and had made careful plans for disposing of it when the time came. Almost routinely, they would see that it was buried in some obscure committee and never allowed to reach the floor of the House. But now the strategy they had proposed to use would not serve. Cannon's ruling on the previous day—and no matter if it had been overturned by the House—had given Norris and his Insurgents the opening for which they had waited.

"We have never been confronted with so critical a situation as now!" moaned Jacob Fasset of New York as the regular Republicans sought for a way out of the trap Norris had sprung.

It was indeed a desperate situation, and desperately Cannon stalled for time.

One of the regulars made a point of order against the introduction of the Norris resolution. Absent members whose votes the leadership could count on were summoned back to the city. Throughout the remainder of that day and all through the night and the following day, the House was engaged in furious debate on whether the resolution was in order. Cannon was in the chair a great part of the time. He left the House occasionally for hurried meals, once for a bath, again to sign some of the papers piling up on his desk in the Speaker's Room. Mostly, he was plotting counterstrategy with his closest associates. Many cigars were smoked.

As the House remained in session and the debate went on, newspapers all over the country played up the drama taking place in the halls of Congress. Telegrams poured in by the hundreds, many of them pleading with the Speaker to resign in order to save the Republican party. "Opportunists!" the old man snorted. It was not he who was splitting the party. The Insurgents were doing that by going over to the Democrats. In fact, he mourned, "The House for the time being had gone a little mad and was no longer governed by reason or established parliamentary procedure." If things were falling apart, he was not to blame.

In the end, Cannon would have to rule on the point of

order. Then it would be up to the House to sustain or override him. Before reaching that point of no return, the Speaker was determined to exhaust every possibility of softening the blow he now grimly expected to fall. On the second day of the debate, a two-hour recess was ordered. Frenzied efforts were made during that brief interval to arrive at a compromise. The Cannon forces proposed removing from the Norris resolution the especially unpalatable provision excluding the Speaker from membership on the Rules Committee. Norris and his little band, consulting with the Democrats, would not agree to this. Cannon would agree to nothing less. The recess ended without an accommodation having been reached.

Cannon had come to a decision, an inevitable decision to his mind, and he at last announced he was ready to rule on the question of whether it was a privilege under the Federal Constitution for a member to offer a resolution, whatever the circumstances, to change the rules of the House.

On Saturday, March 19, the Speaker, his usually genial face haggard and unsmiling, left his official quarters with a small group of trusted friends. They were glumly silent as they proceeded into the House chamber. Just before he went to the Speaker's stand, Cannon turned to his friends, his grizzled chin set. "Boys, it looks as though we're beaten," he told them, "but we'll die game."

In the chair, Cannon cited the precedents that had been compiled for him by the House parliamentarian. He spoke of rulings made by Speakers in the past. He called particular attention to a resolution, almost a duplicate of the one offered by Norris, which had been proposed in the House on December 13, 1876, by Roger Q. Mills, a Texas Democrat. That resolution had been overruled by the Democratic Speaker, Samuel Randall.

"There was criticism, grave criticism, of the rule in those days as there is today," Cannon said, looking reproachfully down at the members from his rostrum, "but no man in that House thought of appealing from a decision so consonant with reason. Planting himself upon the law made for the House by Mr. Speaker Randall, appealing from the passion of this day to the just reason of that day, the Chair sustains the point of order and holds that the resolution is not in order."

It was a ringing conclusion to a solemnly dramatic statement. But the Speaker could not make his ruling stand. Norris immediately appealed from the decision. Amidst confusion and shouting, the Speaker was overruled for the second time in that hectic week. The vote was 182 to 163. The House went ahead at once to vote on the Norris resolution as amended. It carried, 191 to 156, with the aid of 42 Republicans, by no means all of whom could be labeled Insurgents.

Norris, temporarily in charge on the floor, moved to adjourn the session. It was a privileged motion and the Speaker recognized it. But, he said, he had a statement to make and requested that the gentleman from Nebraska withhold his motion for the moment. Norris agreed. Cannon played out the last card in the game of strategy he and a few others had outlined in their closed sessions in the Speaker's Room.

A new majority had been created in the House, Cannon said with stern impassiveness. It was not a Republican majority nor was it a Democratic majority. It was made up of Democrats and Insurgents. The Speaker could, of course, resign and permit this hybrid majority, with which he was not in sympathy, "to choose a Speaker in harmony with its aims and purposes." This he would not do, for two reasons. He stated them.

First, his resignation would cause a contest, probably prolonged in extent, for the speakership and this would tie up all legislative activity to the detriment of the country. Second, a resignation would imply an apology or a confession of weakness, and "the Speaker is not conscious of having done any political wrong." No, he would not resign.

But he was ready, Cannon stated, glaring defiantly at the members on the floor, to entertain a motion that the office of the Speaker be declared vacant. If that were done, the newly created majority—the unspeakable combine of Insurgent Republicans and Democrats—could proceed to name its own Speaker.

Albert Sidney Burleson, a Texas Democrat and something of a maverick, sprang to his feet to offer a motion declaring the speakership vacant. Cannon ruled that the motion was in order and, asking his Republican floor leader to take the Chair, left the House and waited in the Speaker's Room for the vote.

Burleson had acted, as he often did, on his own. His resolution, supported by only nine of the Insurgents, was defeated by a vote of 192 to 155. Norris himself said he viewed Burleson's motion with regret. His purpose had been not to punish an individual but to remove "autocratic powers" from the Speaker's office.

Cannon saw the vote on this resolution as a personal vindication. "When I went back to resume the Chair," he exulted, "I received a demonstration from both sides such as the House had seldom witnessed." So he did; the House of Representatives has often shown itself to be a sentimental institution.

The Norris rules-revising resolution, as finally enacted, had been amended to provide for a ten-member Rules Committee, six from the majority and four from the minority. They were to be selected by the House. The Speaker could not be a member and the committee was to elect its own chairman. The Speaker retained for the time the power to appoint other committees.

Cannon, in the book written for him by Busbey, gave his own rationalization:

"The Insurgents secured a new Committee on Rules and the Speaker was not a member of it. But John Dalzell, who had long been a member of the old committee, was made chairman. The Republicans were all stalwarts, satisfied with the old committee, and the minority members were all Democrats of the old school. There was not an Insurgent on the committee.

"The new committee had an increased membership, divided on party lines as before, and it functioned as had the old committee. The one significant difference was a committee room and a committee clerk to add to the expenses of the House.

[The old Rules Committee had met—where else?—in the Speaker's Room.] Dalzell had been the working member and ruling spirit of the old committee because of his parliamentary knowledge and experience in preparing special rules, and he continued to be the ruling spirit of the new committee as well as its chairman. If anything else was accomplished by the revolution I do not remember."

That was written some years after the event, but it is doubtful that Cannon's memory actually had failed him to such an extent. If the revolt finally accomplished something less than the Insurgents had hoped, it nevertheless reduced the stature of the Speaker more than a little.

Champ Clark was a good enough politician to make use of the Insurgents while he could. The House went ahead to take a series of reform actions that resulted in giving all members, and especially members of the minority, some protection from authoritarianism in the speakership. A discharge rule was adopted, empowering a majority of the House to take bills away from committees if they persisted in failing to report them. The establishment of "Calendar Wednesday," set aside for a call of the House committees, enabled any committee to bring up a bill otherwise blocked from consideration. The minority was given the right to move to recommit any bill before the House voted on its final passage.

Despite Cannon's brave effort to show that he had lost no powers that really mattered, his personal authority over the House had been sharply curtailed. This was due not alone to the changes in the rules but also to the fact that, having been successfully challenged, his voice no longer bore the whipcrack of personal power. His simple yes or no was not now sufficient to decide the fate of a bill. He could still do many things, but he could not again run the House as a one-man show.

There was still fight in the old man. In June, 1910, after the House took the radical step of passing the discharge rule, Cannon turned the Chair over to a colleague and took the floor for a pugnacious diatribe against Democrats and Insurgents. Waving his hands in the windmill fashion of old, his voice rising to a hoarse shout, he denied the charge that he had acted as a dictator, paid his special compliments to Victor Murdock, and called down the wrath of political gods of the past on the Republicans who had joined with the Democratic enemy in voting for the discharge rule.

He was not optimistic about the way things were going. In a speech before his fellow-spirits of the National Association of Manufacturers in the spring of that year, Cannon warned against the power that had been attained in Congress by "our Democratic-Populist friends." Unless the Republicans were kept in control in the November election, he predicted darkly, "the uplift magazines and the college professors" would take over and a severe economic depression would almost surely follow.

In October, fighting hard to keep his own House seat, he wrote a friend: "I seek no personal vindication from anybody except my constituents. If they vindicate me by an election, I will form a part of the majority or minority in the House, as the case may be, but I will keep the Republican faith." He kept the faith and he did win, although by less than his usual heavy majority. But the Democrats gained control of the House, taking 228 seats to 161 for the Republicans, and put Champ Clark in as Speaker.

When Cannon left the speakership at the end of the Sixty-first Congress, he refused to accept the post of minority leader for his party. He moved from the Speaker's Room into the House Office Building, which later was to be named for him, and assumed the duties of an ordinary member of Congress. He was the ranking Republican on the Appropriations Committee, however, and in that capacity he largely abandoned his role of Treasury watchdog, urging on the Democrats higher expenditures than they wanted.

He was defeated for re-election in 1912, a year of disaster for the Republican party, but the voters of his district sent him back to Congress two years later. They kept him there until 1923, when the veteran of forty-six years of service in the House voluntarily retired at the age of eighty-seven and went back to Danville to stay.

In Cannon's latter years in the House, the bitterness that had enveloped him for a time after his defeat by the Insurgents faded away. He again became, as he was always meant to be, one of the most popular members of the House—kind, talkative, a good companion, generous in his advice to newcomers, at home with everybody and never boring others with tales of the days when he commanded the House and the House obeyed. "A hundred years from now," he predicted jocosely in a House speech, "they will say, 'It does appear that there was a man from Illinois by the name of Cannon, but I don't know much about him. There was another man by the name of Cannon in Congress from Utah, and it was said he had seventeen wives.' "

It was Uncle Joe, not the Czar, who spoke as he returned to Danville: "In saying goodbye to public life, I think I can honestly say that the nation is the strongest in the world, and the people are growing better and better every day."

He died in Danville on November 12, 1926, at the age of ninety.

4

Some students of American politics have advanced the theory that Cannon was largely responsible for the creation of the welfare state in this country. They contend that the extent of public and congressional reaction to his period of power opened the way for Woodrow Wilson's New Freedom and Franklin Delano Roosevelt's New Deal. Blair Bolles, a Cannon biographer, thought the "experiment in heroism" undertaken by the Speaker "ushered the United States politically and intellectually into the twentieth century." And William Allen White wrote, "Emma Goodman, in her palmiest days, never made as many anarchists as Cannon."

Whether or not this theory is wholly acceptable, it is certain that the reformers of the time did need a personified villain, and Cannon obligingly cast himself in that role.

Not that he was ever a villain in his own eyes—far from it. Believing as he did that the United States was the greatest success in the world, he was bound to use his power as Speaker of the House to hamstring those who wanted to tamper with the existing system. Proposals for this kind of meddling were, to him, divided into two categories: those that were harmful and those that were useless. Even his favoritism toward the big corporations, the "trusts," had its origin in the fact that they were part of the status quo. His resistance to change served their interests by helping them to retain the advantages they had gained since the Civil War, but that was only incidental. The big point was to keep things as they were. It was well remarked of Cannon that if he had been present at the caucus on Creation he would have been staunchly loyal to Chaos.

This was the Cannon who said: "While the critic has his place, he does very little to help make the wheels go round. He may get into the clouds and spread a mist of hazy talk about progressive ideas, or go down in the mire throwing mud at everybody, but we need men who will keep on the level and deal with realities to work out definite plans." It was the Cannon who, as chairman of the Appropriations Committee, told the other members, "You think it is my business to make appropriations, but it is not. It is to prevent their being made." And this was his policy except when the Democrats controlled the committee. Then—capriciously and perhaps chuckling to himself—he had done everything he could to give the opposition the spendthrift label.

He permitted one experiment with the newfangled during his service as chairman of Appropriations, and never quite got over its failure. He was somehow persuaded to accede to a request by Samuel P. Langley of the Smithsonian Institution for ten thousand dollars to build a flying machine. The machine crashed into the Potomac River on its first attempt at flight. The "Watchdog of the Treasury" was the butt of considerable ridicule, and the experience hardened his stand against that which had not already been tried and proven.

His fiscal conservatism was personal as well as governmental. He never forgot that shortly after he first came to Washington he had been talked into investing a thousand dollars of his own money in the scheme of an alchemist to turn base metal into gold. That money having gone down the drain, he later scathingly rejected suggestion that he make a modest investment in the company that was to become American Telephone and Telegraph. He also turned down another proposal that he get in on the ground floor when the Mergenthaler typesetting machine was being developed. But, he said, defensively, he "might have lost a dozen fortunes by accepting similar offers."

Cannon held all his life to a heartfelt conviction that the Democratic party was literally unfit to govern the country. This belief was basic in his political faith; it was unarguable. The Democrats were irrepressible advocates of a showy and unstable governmental policy, and it was natural that trouble should always follow their coming into power. They had no regard for doing things as they always had been done. Their own President, Wilson, first Chief Executive to address Congress in person, spoke "from the throne of the Speaker of the House," and in doing so "smashed a precedent of one hundred years and followed one of the thousand years of autocratic government before the days of Washington and Jefferson." Cannon writhed at such a spectacle.

Even his hayseed pose—which he maintained long after it had any validity, at least in the political field—grew out of his resistance to change. He used the image he had of himself as a man of the people to strengthen the authority he wielded over the representatives of the people.

His essential vulgarity was not, however, a pose at all. It was, declared Mark Sullivan, "of the spirit" and "at once the unconscious and the deliberate expression of his personality." His contempt toward art, literature, architecture, the niceties of life, was wholly unfeigned. It was instinctive. He was never caught reading a book, and Fuller, who saw him in action as Speaker, considered him "probably the most unimaginative man in public life."

Cannon was quite capable of deliberately going out of his way to prove his uncouthness. At a White House dinner for Prince Chio Tao, the brother of the regent of China, a suggestion was made to the Speaker that he walk across the room to be introduced to the honor guest. He replied in a loud voice, "It goes against my pride for an American freeborn citizen to cross a room to meet a heathen Chinee." He again embarrassed his presidential host—it was Taft—the same evening when he assumed a more cordial attitude toward the guest by sitting with an arm thrown around the royal shoulders as he regaled him with political anecdotes. Cannon made sure the prince got the point of each joke by jabbing him in the ribs at the climax.

The newspapers were fond of publishing such stories about the Speaker. Uncle Joe would never change, they said.

But the country had changed and was continuing to change. The kind of economic freedom the average American had enjoyed during the decades when free, or practically free, land was in ample supply was being lost. It was no longer easy for a man to "pick up and move West" when trouble closed in on him. More people were living in cities. During the first ten years of the new century the urban population had increased by 34 per cent, the rural population by only 11 per cent. Cities brought a new type of industrial and economic structure, which at times pressed hard on free-moving spirits and resulted in the unrest of which Cannon saw the "demagogues" taking advantage.

As for himself, he would not admit the changes that were occurring. He looked back to his boyhood on a newly created farm in rural Illinois as an ideal time, a time when there was "no eight-hour law, no child labor law, no maternity law, no compulsory school law in that settlement." Cannon had said of McKinley that he kept his ear so close to the ground that from time to time it became filled with grasshoppers. But the Speaker, wily politician as he was, did not have his own ears open to the winds of change that eventually blew down his power house.

What had been his strength became a fatal weakness, and resulted at last in losing for him the support not alone of the Insurgents but also of many conservative Republicans. As Bolles remarked, he was giving conservatism a bad name—he, the essence, the very symbol, of conservatism. He had become an anachronism of which the Republican party must rid itself.

The newspapers were right in believing he would never change. He never did. He always had known his own mind. As a young Quaker who had married outside the church, he was directed by a member of the Friends to get up in meeting and express regret. He refused. "I'm damned if I'm sorry," he blurted, "and I'm damned if I will say I am."

In later years he was not in the least sorry about his political demeanor. Years after he had left the Speaker's chair, he still saw himself as "a goat" who had had "to take the responsibility for doing or refusing to do something in the face of criticism." "Nowadays," he added with scorn, "a Speaker is expected to be nothing more than a Sunday School teacher, to pat all the good little boys on the head and turn the other cheek when the bad boys want to use him as a target for their bean shooters."

Cannon was a relic in his own time. Yet, there was more, much more, to him than that.

In his operation of the House, he took the available rules and applied them ruthlessly in a way that he believed would help to keep the country he loved on an even keel. Any man in power with the courage of his convictions—and Cannon had that in full measure—would surely have done the same. He may have grown cynical during his long political career; he was never accused of being corrupt. In his first campaign for district attorney he learned that "in politics as in everything else a man has to depend on his general reputation for square dealing," and that was the reputation he had in the House.

He knew but one political master, the standpat Republican

party. "It's a damned good thing to remember in politics," he advised, "to stick to your party and never attempt to buy the favor of your enemies at the expense of your friends."

To the end of his days, when interviewed by reporters, Cannon was likely at some point to tilt his head back and recite a few lines of doggerel he had once come across in a newspaper:

> I'm thankful that the sun and the moon
>   Are both hung up so high
> That no pretentious hand can stretch
>   And pull them from the sky.
>
> If they were not, I have no doubt
>   But some reforming ass
> Would recommend to take them down
>   And light the world with gas.

In two memorable sentences, spoken at a time when he was at the height of his power, Cannon summed up a lifetime of conviction: "Everything is all right out West and around Danville. The country don't need any legislation."

V

Man of the House

THE WIFE OF A MEMBER of the House of Representatives once asked Speaker Sam Rayburn, as a long session of Congress dragged on, when he expected the House to adjourn. The Speaker responded by telling of a farmer who was leading a restive bull along a country lane by a rope looped around the animal's neck. He met a neighbor, who demanded, "Hey, where are you going with that bull?" "I don't know," replied the farmer. "Ask the bull."

Telling a friend about the incident, the congressional wife said, "I thought I *was* asking the bull."

She was right. She had put her question to the person who knew the House of Representatives as nobody else in that institution's history.

1

Sam Rayburn could read the sentiment of the House as other men read their morning newspapers. He devoted all of his energies and nearly all his waking time to the business of the House. He was a member there for almost half a century. He was Speaker for seventeen years, a record more than twice as long as that set by Henry Clay in the early part of the nation's history. He was House floor leader for the Democratic party in four Congresses. For six years he was chairman of the Committee on Interstate and Foreign Commerce, the panel that handled much of Franklin D. Roosevelt's precedent-shattering New Deal legislation.

This House he knew so intimately was his life and, in his words, his love. In the end, it was almost his only love. During his nearly fifty years in that chamber he served beside some three thousand Representatives, and he knew most of them well. A few of the three thousand he considered great statesmen. Most were hard-working and conscientious. There were but a few who, in Rayburn's opinion, should never have been sent to the House.

"Good or bad, run-of-the-mill or outstanding, they were selected by the voters of their districts and they deserved to be heard," he said. "They brought to the House the opinions, hopes, dreams, and prejudices of the people who had chosen them. They were representative, in the most literal sense of the word, of their people."

The Speaker sometimes told with amusement—mixed with a sort of grim approval—about a new member from a district where, Rayburn said delicately, "the level of education was not as high as it might have been." This man had some rough edges and he knew it. He told the Speaker, "I don't belong here. I don't know what's going on and never will. But you'll never get rid of me because I'm just like my folks at home."

The story was used by Rayburn to explain his feeling that, ultimately and in historical perspective, the House was always truly representative in fact as well as in name. That was what made it a governmental institution second to no other. "This," the Speaker told the membership in a 1957 speech, "is the highest theater that anyone plays in upon this earth today." He had always felt that way. When, as a young Representative, he was urged to give up the House and run for the United States Senate from Texas, he refused, saying, "The House of Representatives should be high enough for any man's ambition."

Rayburn was Speaker during all or part of four administra-

tions, those of Franklin Delano Roosevelt, Truman, Eisenhower, and Kennedy. He was in the House during the adminis-
trations of four other Presidents, Wilson, Harding, Coolidge
and Hoover. Personally a modest and wholly unassuming man,
he jealously upheld the prerogatives and prestige of House
membership. "I never served *under* any President," he once
snapped back at an interviewer who had made such an implica-
tion. "I served *with* eight."

As democratically unpretentious as the House itself, he
wielded his vast power quietly, often almost invisibly. In any
given session of Congress there were certain to be several members who looked more like a Speaker of the House than Rayburn did. He had neither the appearance nor the demeanor of
a professional politician, much less a Texas politician. He was
short in stature—five feet, six inches—and solidly built, never
running to fat. He wore dark suits and black hats. When he
was hatless he revealed a head bald as a peeled onion, about
which he was surprisingly sensitive. His rubbery, expressive
face, dominated by dark brown eyes, customarily had a sober
look, and he gained a widespread reputation for being gruff,
even irascible. This reputation was partly deserved; it was
partly a busy man's protection against idle encroachments upon
his time. Though Rayburn might often be brusque, he was not
only a kindly man but, basically, a friendly man as well.

It was with both kindliness and friendliness, as well as with
firmness, that he dealt with members of the House. "I have
never hated any man," he observed, "although I have been
temporarily provoked with several."

No one would have picked him out of a crowd as the second
most politically powerful figure in the United States—and there
were times when, in everything but official title, he would have
had to be accounted the first. His appearance was in general
that of a moderately successful storekeeper in a small town.
Yet he was for seventeen years leader of the House of Representatives. He was not its master as Reed had been, not its
tough-minded driver as Cannon had been. But he was without

challenge its leader, a man who was able amazingly often to arrange matters so that his party colleagues in the House sought reasons why they should follow him instead of reasons why they should balk.

How did he do it? Rayburn doubted that any leader could explain how he leads. "I do know," he said, "that in the case of the House the Speaker has to be utterly responsive to the waves of sentiment rolling out from its members. If he does not have the *feel* of the House, he is lost and he might as well quit."

He had that "feel" to a superlative degree. It was said of him that from the moment he walked into the hall of the House at the beginning of a day's session he could know the mood of the members—which might be markedly different from yesterday's mood—and foretell what could be expected of them that day. There was nothing mystic about this intuitive sense of the House. It was developed through years of dealing with all the varied types of representatives the American voters sent to Washington. It grew also out of Rayburn's consciously conducted and never-ending search for information about all aspects of all matters concerning the business of the House.

The door of his office was always open to members, as he told them from the first day they came to Congress. Day after day they entered that door, not only to pour out their problems to the sympathetic Speaker, but also, wittingly or not, to feed him the bits and pieces of knowledge he must have to keep him abreast of the House or, preferably, a step ahead of it. Newspaper people were also a prime source of information. They came to see him frequently and to those he trusted he talked with the utmost freedom—and, to their frustration, almost always off the record. More important, the newsmen talked to him, helping him to add a piece or two to the jigsaw puzzle that he was eternally putting together in his mind. His most common parting words to visitors were, "Let me know if you hear anything."

Then there was his famous "Board of Education." Rayburn

did not like this term as applied to the small evening gatherings held in a one-room office hidden away on the first floor of the Capitol. Despite his feeling, the sessions were aptly named. They were educational in the most practical sense possible.

Old and trusted friends in the House—and occasionally an outsider if Rayburn had known him a long time—would meet "downstairs," as the Speaker referred to the hideaway, to plot legislative strategy or simply to exchange the political news and gossip by which they lived. Republican leaders sometimes would be on hand, and it was in this room that accommodations were reached between the two parties on many matters relating to the operation of the House. A few Senators were regular attendants at the meetings, notable among them Lyndon Johnson, Rayburn's long-time friend and protégé, who kept coming even after he became Vice-President. Harry Truman was at a "Board of Education" meeting the April evening he was abruptly called to the White House to receive the news that Roosevelt was dead and he was President. If a new member of the House was invited "downstairs," it was a sure sign that he was beginning to figure in the future plans of the leadership.

These friendly, informal sessions, a few men chatting together casually in a small room, constituted a main source of Rayburn's uncanny ability to know what the House was going to do even before the House itself knew. Members were encouraged to let down their hair in this atmosphere. Drinks were available. Political jokes were enjoyed, although off-color stories were taboo. Nobody pressured anybody else here, and nobody talked any foolishness either. It was a picture, even if not a conventional one, of professional politicians at work.

Rayburn, operating without the rules that had given Reed and Cannon so much authority over the House, eventually became the most influential of all Speakers. He did not try to coerce members to his way of thinking. "I am not much of a hand," he said, "to pound the table and insist on having my own way when everybody else disagrees with me." Yet nobody doubted that he would fight with every ounce of his strength for principles in which he believed and for legislation which he favored.

Rayburn, having been a member of the House for so long, benefited enormously and continuously from the camaraderie of that body. He understood and made use of the instinctive togetherness of the House in matters affecting itself.

"When a new member comes in, he will find his colleagues are pulling for him," he said. "They want him to make good. If he handles himself well in his first speech or in his committee duties, they are glad and they tell him so. But if he falls down in his work or fails to pull his weight in committee or becomes self-important, that fact is noted. If he keeps on the same way, eventually the other members will have no more to do with him than they can help."

That was fair, Rayburn thought, the House being a place where every member was given a chance to show the stuff of which he was made.

As to his own leadership, history, the Speaker believed, indicated that the House had always been willing to listen to and to follow the man who was reasonable, who understood what he was about, the man with common sense. "If you have common sense," he said many times, "you have all the sense there is. But that's not enough—you have to use it."

The man from Bonham, Texas, had a full measure of what he called common sense, a full measure of what the House recognized over a period of many years as the ability to lead. Rayburn always knew what he was doing and, to a far greater extent than most men, why he was doing it. He was a man who did not admire uncalled-for complexity in either word or deed. A new member of the House once asked the Speaker if he was doing too much talking on the floor of the House.

"Yes," Rayburn replied.

"Well," pressed the freshman, "what should I do about it?"

"Quit it," said Rayburn.

Henry Clay had led the House by the force of his personal

magnetism, Reed by vastly superior brain power, Cannon by a combination of bulldozing and good-fellowship backed up by rigidly restrictive rules. Rayburn led the House—and for nearly as long a period as the three earlier Speakers combined—by friendly persuasiveness, a desire to be helpful to members, rock-bound integrity, and by reaping the dividends of service so extended that, at the last, almost every political figure of importance in the Democratic party owed the Speaker favors in return for favors received.

His friend of many years and his successor as Speaker, John W. McCormack of Massachusetts, summed it up in a heartfelt eulogy: "Sam Rayburn had an intense love for the House of Representatives. During his lifetime as Speaker, more than twice as long as any other Speaker, he never permitted his great abilities, his amazing knowledge of the rules and of parliamentary law, to carry him beyond the rules of the House and the dictates of the Constitution. Sam Rayburn would never in his life for as much as a single moment have violated the established practices of the House, and he always insisted that the dignity and the prerogatives of the House be maintained."

It was a meaningful tribute from one House man to another.

2

Sam Rayburn was born near Kingston, Tennessee, January 6, 1882, the eighth of eleven children of William Marion and Martha Waller Rayburn. His birthplace was a log cabin built by his father. His parents gave him, as he later said, the "highfalutin brand" of Samuel Taliafero, the first part of which he shortened and the second part of which he abandoned as soon as he was old enough to think about such matters.

The family moved to Texas when Sam was five years old, and settled on a forty-acre farm in the Flag Springs community in Fannin County. The move to the outskirts of Bonham, in the same county, came later. That northeastern section of Texas was a desolate and sparsely settled area, the level, empty earth stretching away from the farm on all sides. Despite the size of the Rayburn family, young Sam had a lonely boyhood. "On Sunday I used to sit on the fence in front of the house," he recalled in after-years, "and wish and wish that somebody would ride by on a horse or in a buggy—just anybody to relieve the monotony, just somebody to see and wave at."

He attended a two-teacher country school, and when he finished what was offered there he was an eighteen-year-old youth determined to go on to college. He had saved five dollars, which was more than enough to pay his railroad fare to the nearby town of Commerce where Mayo Normal College was located. His father accompanied him to the station and waited until the train came in. As Sam was about to get aboard, his father handed him twenty-five dollars. "God knows how he had saved it," Rayburn would wonder in talking of that day, remembering the hard times, the meager forty acres of the farm, and the large family the parents had to feed and clothe.

At Mayo Normal he worked to pay his way. He swept the floors, rang the college bell, eagerly attacked whatever odd jobs were available. He dropped out one year to teach school and to earn enough money to complete his college studies.

He returned to teaching school, that being what a young man with a Bachelor's degree was most likely to do in the rural Texas of that era. However, the young man had one day heard a speech by a spellbinding Texas politician named Joseph Weldon Bailey, a United States Senator, and his mind had become set on a political career. In 1906, when he was twenty-four, Rayburn filed his candidacy for a seat in the state House of Representatives. He told a friend that he wanted to spend about three terms in the legislature and planned to be elected Speaker of the House. "After that," he announced solemnly, "I am going to run for Congress and be elected."

He followed his blueprint precisely, adding to it while in the legislature by obtaining a law degree from the University of Texas. In his third term he became Speaker of the Texas House, the youngest man—at twenty-nine—who had ever been chosen for that position. In 1912 he was a candidate for the

United States House of Representatives. He won the Democratic nomination over seven opponents in the summer of that year, and, in that Fourth District of Texas where Republicans were in scant supply, was officially elected in November.

The new member, a Democrat by earnest conviction as well as by birth and environment, was fortunate in entering Congress just as the Democratic party was emerging from a long period of wandering in the political wilderness. Woodrow Wilson, the college president who had successfully turned his attention to politics and become the governor of New Jersey, was inaugurated President of the United States on March 4, 1913. He was the first Democrat to occupy the White House in sixteen years. The serious young man from Texas, just two months past his thirty-first birthday, witnessed the inaugural, and spoke of the event ever afterward as one of the high points of his life.

Speaker Champ Clark of Missouri administered the oath of office to Sam Rayburn on April 7 when Wilson called Congress into special session to receive his New Freedom program. The Sixty-third Congress was to remain in continuous session for a year and a half, until October 24, 1914. Members of the House of Representatives in that Congress included two future Vice-Presidents, John Nance Garner of Texas and Alben Barkley of Kentucky, and five future Speakers: Frederick Huntington Gillett of Massachusetts, Garner, Henry T. Rainey of Illinois, Joseph W. Byrns of Tennessee, and Rayburn himself. And it included many other men who, with Rayburn, were to help write innumerable pages of political history during their service in the House.

After the Census of 1910, the House had reached its full size of 435 members. There were so many Representatives that in the year Rayburn took office it was no longer possible to provide them with individual desks in the chamber. The desks were taken out, and since then only unassigned seats have been provided on the House floor, members occupying any vacant chair on their side of the aisle.

Rayburn had no illusions about his status as a freshman

member. He knew there were a great many men ahead of him. But he was not envious. For the present it was enough for him simply to be among such men. "I didn't envy them their positions," he said afterward. "I was willing to wait my turn."

He began at once to get ready for his "turn." Garner, a fellow Texan who already had been in Congress for ten years, took a fancy to Rayburn, and Garner even then was in a position to help members he liked. The older man, popular with both the Democrats and the Republicans, was close to the House leadership. He advised Rayburn that the most powerful House committees were Ways and Means, on which he himself proposed to take the place that had been vacated by Rayburn's predecessor, and Interstate and Foreign Commerce. William C. Adamson of Georgia, chairman of the latter committee, was Garner's close friend. In short order, Rayburn was assigned to the Committee on Interstate and Foreign Commerce. He was never on any other committee during his long House career.

The young Texan made friends readily. He moved into the old Cochran Hotel, where many other members lived, and there he was a regular attendant at a superb school of political science. "Each night after supper," Rayburn recalled, "most of these men would pull their chairs together at the end of the big old lobby and for several hours they would explore together in serious candor the great issues of the hour." The Representative of the Fourth District of Texas listened with rapt attention.

Among the participants in these sessions was Cordell Hull, who had come to the House from Tennessee in 1907. Hull was one of the first friends Rayburn made in Washington. Chairman Adamson of the Interstate and Foreign Commerce Committee, father of the eight-hour day for American labor, grew very fond of the young man and came to depend on him heavily in important committee matters. Hatton Sumners, another Texan who was serving his first term in the Sixty-third Congress, became an intimate; he later was chairman of the House Judiciary Committee. And, of course, the seasoned and colorful Garner was always available to his younger friend. Thus, from the first, Rayburn was in close association with many of the men who in his time would come to form a power structure of great force in the affairs of the nation.

If anyone foresaw this, he did not record his prediction. According to Bascom N. Timmons, who started his journalistic career in Washington at about this time, Rayburn's new colleagues did not consider him brilliant. Said Timmons, "He was regarded as a possessor of all the solid rural virtues in a Congress in which nearly all leaders were of rural origin." And Timmons listed those virtues: "He was friendly, able, honest, industrious, serious, unhurried, and calm." They were traits that Rayburn retained all his life. He was never spectacular; he was always solid.

For a man who after he became Speaker was given to advising neophytes to hold their tongues until they had been around for some time, Rayburn made his first speech remarkably early in his first term—only one month after he had taken his seat. He took note of the fact that it was early.

"As a new member of this body," he said, "I, of course, feel that I should have regard for the long-established custom of the House, which in a measure demands that discussion of questions shall be left to the more mature members. But I feel that as a Representative of more than 200,000 citizens of the Fourth Congressional District of Texas, I should be allowed to break in a measure whatever of this custom remains, and exercise a constitutional right to speak my sentiments on this floor and refuse to be relegated to that lockjawed ostracism typical of the dead past."

His subject was the Underwood tariff bill, which lowered the high tariffs imposed by the Republican-passed Payne-Aldrich law and which also carried an amendment providing for an income tax in accordance with the recently enacted Sixteenth Amendment to the Constitution. Rayburn had consulted with a few of his friends about the content of the speech, but it was his own work and written out in his own hand. He used no oratorical flourishes, but the forceful earnestness of the stocky young man with the sober face, a young man who knew precisely what he wanted to say in this maiden speech, drew the attention of the House.

"I came to this body a few weeks ago with childlike enthusiasm and confidence," he declared. "It has always been my ambition since childhood to live such a life that one day my fellow citizens would call me to membership in this popular branch of the greatest lawmaking body in the world. Out of their confidence and partiality they have done this. It is now my sole purpose here to help enact such wise and just laws that our common country will by virtue of these laws be a happier and more prosperous country."

Rayburn, even in those early days of his career, had a kind of simple, homely eloquence. He had done a great deal of study in preparation for this speech, and his presentation of the traditional Democratic view of the tariff made an impression on some of the far-sighted leaders of the House. They began to keep an eye on this young friend of Garner.

One man who kept an eye on him was Champ Clark. The politically experienced Missourian one day in 1916 asked Rayburn to come over to see him in his office. There Clark talked to him with friendly bluntness about the young Texan's future. The Speaker told Rayburn he was convinced that, assuming he could hold onto his congressional seat, he should be able to attain any position in the House he wanted. That included the speakership, Clark said. However, Rayburn had weaknesses, one of which was that he simply did not know enough about the governmental history of his own country. Clark, suggesting a course of reading, recommended especially the writings of Thomas Jefferson and biographies of the early Presidents, Washington, John Adams, John Quincy Adams, and Andrew Jackson. Also, the Speaker added, Rayburn would do well to study the legislative methods of effective House leaders of the past.

"It was about the best advice anyone ever gave me," Rayburn remembered.

He did all the reading Clark had prescribed and lengthened the list. He found particular value in the writings and speeches of Woodrow Wilson, for whom he had a profound admiration. Also, rather oddly for such a down-the-line Democrat, he conceived a great respect for William McKinley as he dug into the history of the time when that most conservative of all Republicans was a starred actor on the political stage. Rayburn told his friend Timmons that McKinley came close to being the ideal legislator and was a much underrated President.

It was not difficult for Rayburn to find time for his reading. The rural district he represented made comparatively few demands on him, and his office staff consisted of only one clerk. The Texan was no time waster. His usual recreation was playing dominoes with Hull and other colleagues in the evening. He eschewed the cutthroat poker games of which Garner and his cronies were so fond. He had few dates with women, seeming not much interested in them.

Altogether, the young Representative led a quiet life. In the latter days of the Wilson Administration, he left his hotel and took bachelor quarters with two other Texas congressmen. Later, he moved into an apartment in a sedate residential hotel and lived there, when he was in Washington, the last thirty years of his life. He spent a minimum of time and thought on the mechanics of living, although he liked comfortable surroundings, good food and, in reasonable quantities, good drink. He loved the company of a few close friends—and, most of all, he loved politics and the House of Representatives.

In keeping with the innate dignity that was one of his chief characteristics, Rayburn lived his personal life within himself. Until after his death only a few persons knew that he had been married. His marriage took place in the fall of 1927, when he was forty-five years old, and it was to Metze Jones, a Texas woman of twenty-seven. She was the sister of Marvin Jones, one of the congressmen with whom Rayburn had shared bachelor quarters some years before and who later became Chief Judge of the United States Court of Claims in Washington. The marriage lasted only about three months. Beyond writing to a friend in Bonham that he had made a mistake, Rayburn never referred to his marriage. The few persons, including two or three newsmen, who knew about it respected his silence on the subject and never brought it up. He and Jones remained close friends until Rayburn's death.

In 1920 so many Democrats went down to defeat—even Hull —that Rayburn, who always had an opponent but always won, jumped far up the House seniority ladder. He became the ranking Democratic member of the Interstate and Foreign Commerce Committee. Later in the twenties, when Garner was named Democratic floor leader, Rayburn was one of the inside coterie that planned party strategy and tactics in the House.

Garner's group was able at times to lure enough Republicans into voting with them to make possible the amendment of measures that the Democrats considered overly favorable to business interests. On the whole, however, it was a period of frustration for any House Democrat hoping to get ahead. Rayburn, who had made his first House speech on behalf of a bill to lower tariffs, was especially vexed by the failure of his and other Democrats' efforts to prevent a tariff increase in 1929 and again by the passage of the Fordney-McCumber act the following year.

The pattern of the Texan's governmental convictions had become clear during his first five terms in Congress. When he announced for re-election in the spring of 1922, Rayburn placed before his constituents a resumé of legislative proposals he had supported, with major attention to measures affecting the farm and farm-dependent people who made up most of the population of his district.

The list included: exemption of farmers' organizations from the Sherman Anti-Trust Act; expanding educational facilities for farm boys and girls; the income tax law; the Underwood Tariff Act; a Federal Reserve act expanding the volume of currency and permitting farmers to borrow money from banks

on notes secured by staple agricultural products and on improved farm lands; a law to curb gambling in cotton and to
regulate the transactions of the cotton exchanges; an act establishing a system of twelve farm-loan banks; Federal assistance
for road improvement; creation of the Federal Trade Commission; and the vocational education act.

Some of these praiseworthy measures, Rayburn complained,
had been weakened by the Republicans, but his support of them
was his record and he stood before the voters on that record.

Times were bad for farmers that year and Rayburn had a
hard campaign. Two hours after the returns started coming in
on the night of the primary election, he studied the tally sheet
on which precinct votes were being recorded and, in dismay,
told a friend, "I have lost this race."

He won, but by a majority much smaller than usual. According to his biographer, C. Dwight Dorough, "some political
historians around Bonham" considered that this campaign
"marked the beginning of Sam Rayburn's emergence from politician to statesman." In any case, his victory two years later was
substantial; two years after that, in 1926, he did not even have
an opponent, which was the first time that had happened.

Things were looking up in the House, too. Even before
1930, although the Republicans continued to hold a majority
and were provided with strong leadership by Speaker Nicholas
Longworth, the Democrats, harassing the Hoover Administration, drew some liberal Republicans in with them on various
issues. Nevertheless, in the November elections, the Republicans won the House for the seventh time in a row. It was close,
though—so close that before Congress met in December, 1931,
the deaths of several Republicans gave the Democrats a majority
of four.

Thin as it was, that majority gave the organization of the
House to the Democrats. Garner was elected Speaker, Rayburn
became chairman of the Interstate and Foreign Commerce Committee, and the House majority headed into two years of determined political effort to bring about the downfall of the Hoover

Administration and a complete takeover by the Democrats in 1932.

Garner himself was a candidate, apparently a serious candidate, for the Democratic nomination for President. The Texas Democratic Convention instructed the state delegation for him, and elected Rayburn his campaign manager and delegation chairman. Garner also won a primary contest in California, defeating both Alfred E. Smith and Franklin D. Roosevelt. The trouble was, as Rayburn privately said, the campaign manager was far more interested than the candidate.

At the Democratic National Convention in Chicago, Garner authorized Rayburn by telephone from Washington to release his delegates when, after three ballots, it became clear that he had no chance of winning. Against heavy opposition, Rayburn maneuvered the Texas delegation into supporting Roosevelt. With California going along, Roosevelt was nominated on the fourth ballot. Garner, somewhat against his will, received the nomination for Vice-President.

As the future was to show, the events of this convention were of far more lasting significance to Rayburn than to Garner. Up to this time, in both Texas and Washington, Rayburn had been just another congressman, even if one who was marked by the leadership for attention and advancement. He had spent his time either on the job in the House or at home among his own people. He had played no large role, nor sought to play one, in party affairs in Texas. This was to be the case no longer. Dating from the 1932 convention, the man from Bonham became a figure of steadily increasing importance in Texas Democratic councils. Since he represented the national party's viewpoint, with which a great many Texas Democrats were rarely in accord, he was also a figure around whom political controversy increasingly swirled.

He brought to his work as a member of Congress a sense of urgency growing out of his conviction that something had to be done for the people of the country and the New Deal was doing it. The Texan had seen the banks closing down in Bonham, Sherman, Greenville, Terrell, Whitesboro, Whitewright, Van Alstyne—in all the towns in his district. He had known farmers whose farms had been sold out from under them. He had seen small-town merchants and manufacturers tumbling into bankruptcy, the auction signs going up in front of their stores, their flour mills, their cotton gins. He knew what a depression meant to the people he saw every day when he was at home. He was committed to helping the home folks whenever and however he could.

In the House, Rayburn headed the committee that received many of the basic New Deal legislative measures. Interstate and Foreign Commerce had become an exceedingly powerful committee after the overthrow of Speaker Joe Cannon's dictatorial regime. The Republican chairman at that time was James R. Mann, Cannon's floor leader, who moved quickly and with a sure hand to increase the scope of the committee. He brought under its jurisdiction the railroads, aviation, navigation, the Coast Guard, the Panama Canal, lighthouses, the Federal Trade Commission, the Federal Power Commission, public health, and other matters vitally affecting the economy of the country. Rayburn simply inherited the far-ranging instrument of power that Mann had built. As a result, he became Roosevelt's active partner in bringing much of the New Deal to life.

Under his chairmanship, the committee set out to report to the House the legislation that would change the concept of American government for all time. In that first New Deal year, Rayburn sponsored the Securities Act of 1933 and the railroad holding company bill. In 1934, his committee reported, and he pushed to passage, measures creating the Securities and Exchange Commission to regulate the stock exchanges and the Federal Communications Commission to regulate in the public interest the use of the air waves. In 1935, he was flung into the hardest fight he had yet known when he sponsored the Public Utility Holding Company Act.

All these measures were the subjects of extensive hearings by the Interstate and Foreign Commerce Committee, and Rayburn presided over the hearings. He spent long hours in study to acquire adequate knowledge of the issues involved. He gave opponents of the bills—and all of the bills met vigorous opposition—full opportunity to set forth their views. On the public utilities holding company bill alone, Rayburn's committee held two months of hearings. The testimony presented filled 2,320 printed pages.

The utilities spent huge sums in their effort to defeat this bill. They hired eminent men to speak against it in public throughout the country and over the radio. They bought newspaper advertising on a massive scale. They set up false-front citizens' organizations to inveigh against the "death sentence" on utility holding companies.

The utility lobby, frantic in its opposition, finally overreached itself in bombarding congressmen with telegrams signed with names picked, at random and without authorization, from telephone books in the lawmakers' home districts. A freshman congressman from Pennsylvania received in two days 816 telegrams calling for the defeat of Rayburn's bill. An investigating committee found that the utility lobby's tactic of snowing Capitol Hill under with such telegrams of protest resulted at the peak of the effort in as many as four thousand wires an hour reaching congressional offices.

The pressure put on Rayburn personally was intense and incredibly bitter. His office was flooded with antagonistic letters. He told friends in later years that it was not uncommon for him to answer a telephone call only to hear some prominent Texan "cuss me out like I was a horse thief." Back home, the utilities promised to move into his district against him in the next election with all the artillery their money would buy. Newspaper editorials castigated him daily as a man who had joined hands with Roosevelt to hurl the nation into socialism.

The bill was finally enacted. None of the dire events predicted by its opponents occurred.

Rayburn moved on to give his close attention in 1936 to obtaining congressional approval of an act setting up the Rural

Electrification Administration. Roosevelt had established this agency by Executive Order in May of the preceding year and had allotted a hundred million dollars to be loaned by the Reconstruction Finance Corporation to electric cooperatives. But only a fraction of the money had been made available. Congress proceeded to pass legislation that would carry out the intent of the Executive Order.

This legislation was close to Rayburn's heart, for he had vivid recollections, unpleasant recollections, of his own boyhood on a farm where the darkness was inadequately lighted by coal-oil lamps, where water had to be pumped by hand, and where home-canned fruits and vegetables and farm produce had to be stored in the storm cellar for whatever primitive refrigeration was available there. Only two years before his birth the New York *Times* had reported, in 1880: "Mr. Edison has converted electricity into a light which does not flicker, which does not require the frequent service of a skilled attendant, and which in quantity and intensity meets the requirements of domestic life." In the very year that Rayburn was born, J. Pierpont Morgan had installed electric lights in his residence in Manhattan. Others had preceded Morgan in this bold step, but the New York financier was the first to have his residence "lit throughout with the new light."

Rayburn had long wanted such good things for his own people. Thus had the New Deal been born, in part, in a Texas countryside unbelievably remote in time and distance from Washington in the mid-thirties.

Even Harold Ickes, FDR's problem-child Secretary of the Interior, who quarreled often with Rayburn (as he quarreled, sooner or later, with everybody), wrote that Roosevelt's most important legislation could not have been enacted without Sam Rayburn.

On January 4, 1937, two days before his fifty-fifth birthday, Rayburn was elected majority floor leader of the House. Speaker Byrns had died near the end of the 1936 session. He was succeeded as Speaker by William B. Bankhead of Alabama, but with adjournment so near no majority leader was named at the time to succeed Bankhead in that post. Representative John J. O'Connor of New York, chairman of the Rules Committee, acted as floor leader during the two weeks that remained.

O'Connor was an active candidate for the place when the new Congress convened, and the talk was that he would have Roosevelt's support. But Rayburn had powerful campaign managers in the persons of Representatives Fred Vinson of Kentucky, later Chief Justice, and Carl Vinson of Georgia, a great force in the House. Furthermore, Vice-President Garner actively backed Rayburn and retorted to those who criticized him for injecting himself into the affairs of the House, "I'm for Rayburn two hundred per cent and I am going to keep working for his election."

Rayburn's victory in the caucus of House Democrats was by a substantial margin. He received 184 votes to 127 for O'Connor.

Floor Leader Rayburn was relieved of committee responsibilities, but he had a multitude of new responsibilities. The 1936 election sweep by the Democrats had brought Republican membership in the House to such a low point that it could not be an effective minority. This created for the Democratic leadership the tender problem that there was not much incentive for cohesiveness among their vulgarly large majority. The usual divisions—North, South; liberal, conservative—existed among the Democrats. This divisiveness was made raucously evident when Roosevelt submitted his proposal to enlarge the membership of the Supreme Court, which had shown a tendency to declare New Deal laws unconstitutional.

The Democratic President's proposal split the Democratic Congress wide apart, leaving the House floor leader an open victim to pressure from both sides—not to mention from the White House. Rayburn's close friend, Hatton Sumners, was chairman of the Judiciary Committee, but he flatly refused to introduce the bill. "Boys," he told Rayburn and others as they glumly left the White House after hearing Roosevelt outline his grand plan, "this is where I cash in my chips."

Another Texan, Maury Maverick of San Antonio (whose grandfather, by refusing to brand his cattle, had made the family name a synonym for a political or any other kind of stray), introduced the bill, but it soon became clear that the measure was doomed. Garner was against it. The powerful Tom Connally, Senator from Texas, was against it. They were but two of many.

The court bill gave Rayburn some of his hardest hours. Friends deserted him on all sides on this issue. One day when he was discussing the matter with Roosevelt, not complaining but simply outlining the situation as it appeared to him, he became aware that the President was paying little attention. "Looky here, Mr. President!" Rayburn exploded. "By God, I'm talking to you. You'd better listen."

Roosevelt eventually did listen long enough to accept the inevitable, and the Supreme Court section of the judiciary bill was eliminated.

During much of the time he was majority leader, Rayburn found himself carrying a double load. Speaker Bankhead's health was poor and he was often absent from the House. In July of 1939, Rayburn was elected Speaker pro tem to act until Bankhead was able to resume his duties.

The bitterness growing out of the court bill and the aftermath of Roosevelt's attempt to "purge" some recalcitrant Democratic congressmen in the 1938 elections combined to give the leadership a House that was hard to handle. Rayburn himself opposed the purge effort. He favored the re-election of all Democrats, contending that the party was sufficiently broad-based to be able to tolerate a few "fractious" members. Some observers thought Rayburn was not tough enough. Even Garner told him, "You've got to get your knuckles bloody once in a while, Sam."

However, that was not Sam Rayburn's way of doing things. During these trying years he was perfecting his chosen method, a method that was natural to him, of leading by persuasion, tact, diplomacy, and a willingness always to listen to the other man's expression of his point of view.

Bankhead died September 15, 1940, and the next day Rayburn was elected Speaker to fill out his term. At the beginning of the first session of the Seventy-seventh Congress, on January 3, 1941, he was elected to his first full term as Speaker of the House.

The man from Texas entered on his duties with better training for the speakership than any man who had ever held that position.

3

During Rayburn's first five years as Speaker, Congress was occupied almost exclusively with problems created by World War II. Although Roosevelt had promised "again and again" in his 1940 campaign for an unprecedented third term that American boys would never be sent to fight in foreign wars, the President was deeply committed to throwing the economic and industrial resources of the United States behind the European allied nations. Before the bombing of Pearl Harbor on December 7, 1941, however, the American people and the United States Congress were by no means unanimous in approving his commitment.

It was the era of the isolationists, the America Firsters, the German-American Bund. Pacifist groups marched to a song called "The Yanks Aren't Coming." Draftees in hastily built military cantonments wrote letters of bitter complaint to their mothers. The Neutrality Act of 1939 was still on the law books, and the Congress had refused the President's appeal for the fortification of Guam and several Pacific bases.

When the Administration submitted legislation providing for the sending of planes, guns, and tanks to England, Rayburn tested the sentiment of the House and reported to Roosevelt that important modifications would have to be made in order to assure passage of the lend-lease bill. The bill was passed, as modified, but Roosevelt continued to be the target of bitter criticism from the isolationists. During these prewar months, the United States was torn by internal dissension. The country was held in the grip of a strange admixture of fear and apathy.

Rayburn experienced a grueling test of his leadership on the preparedness issue less than a year after he had become Speaker. The date was August 12, 1941, and the question up for decision was whether the Selective Service Act should be extended.

The law, which had been enacted in the preceding September, provided for the drafting of 600,000 men into the Army for one year. Now, as the time drew near to discharge the first draftees, parents of many of the affected soldiers called for their release. They were joined in this cry, of course, by the isolationists and their organizations. On the other hand, the War Department warned that to disband the Army might well prove to be disastrous for the nation.

The pressure on Congress was heavy. Congressmen found it hard to resist the pleas of flag-carrying women, with tear-streaked faces, who buttonholed them in their offices and in the corridors of the Capitol to plead that their sons be sent home. The result of the bitter floor fight, carried on for three days, was in doubt to the last moment.

Rayburn conducted his own intensive campaign for votes to extend the draft. He went directly to the members he knew were on the fence and appealed to them on whatever basis he thought likely to be most effective. This was a time, he later admitted, when, if it became necessary, he did not hesitate to make the ultimate plea: "Do this for me. I won't forget it."

The hour of decision arrived. At the conclusion of the tense roll-call vote, the tally clerk handed Rayburn a slip of paper. The Speaker, his face expressionless, glanced at it, and raised his gavel.

"On this vote," he announced tersely, "203 members have voted aye, 202 members have voted no, and the bill is passed."

The poised gavel fell. Rayburn had acted quickly to take advantage of the rule that no member may change his vote once the result of a roll call is announced.

A recapitulation of the vote could be asked, however, and

Dewey Short, Missouri Republican, promptly demanded that. At the conclusion of the review, the Speaker—without pause, almost without punctuation—declared: "No correction in the vote, the vote stands, and the bill is passed, and without objection a motion to reconsider is laid on the table."

And the gavel fell again.

Short protested, demanding reconsideration, but Rayburn replied firmly that he already had announced that "without objection" the motion had been laid on the table.

H. Carl Andersen of Minnesota, aligned with the isolationist forces, arose to declare that the Speaker had not announced the tabling of a motion to reconsider.

"The Chair has twice stated that he did make the statement," Rayburn growled.

"I beg to differ with you," Andersen persisted.

An irritated pink spread over the Speaker's bald head.

"The Chair does not intend to have his word questioned by the gentleman from Minnesota or anyone else," he said coldly, and that was the end of that.

The Texan had given double proof of his leadership qualities. He could get the votes when he had to, and he could maintain his parliamentary position from the rostrum.

After the United States entered the war, although political differences continued and although the anti-Roosevelt cult grew and flourished among a vocal minority, Rayburn had somewhat less difficulty in leading the House to approve the Administration's measures. His job was nevertheless a grinding one. Congress, rolling out legislation to place rigid controls on the civilian economy and to appropriate the huge sums required for waging the war, remained in almost continuous session. Rayburn later heatedly denied that the House was then, or ever, a rubber stamp for the Speaker or that the Speaker was a rubber stamp for the President.

"That rubber stamp stuff never was true," he maintained. "I would go to the White House with other congressional leaders and we would talk things out frankly and openly. Sometimes we agreed and sometimes we disagreed, but in the end we would find more points of agreement than disagreement. And we would get things done. We *had* to get things done."

A substantial portion of the many billions of dollars spent by the United States in fighting the war necessarily was for secret purposes. In such cases, it was up to the Speaker to persuade the House Appropriations Committee to ask for the money and to get it.

Years later, Rayburn told how one day during the war General George Marshall, Chief of Staff, and Secretary of War Stimson, accompanied by Dr. Vannevar Bush, appeared in his office and explained that the United States had to make an atomic bomb—a secret that Roosevelt did not entrust even to his Vice-President. Both haste and secrecy were essential. They wanted the Speaker to arrange for the necessary money to be appropriated with a minimum of discussion.

Rayburn called in his floor leader, John W. McCormack, and Joseph Martin, also of Massachusetts, the minority leader, to share the decision. Rayburn then took the matter up with Clarence Cannon of Missouri, chairman of the Appropriations Committee; Martin approached John Taber of New York, the committee's ranking Republican. Rayburn and Martin asked the two committee members to get the appropriation approved without any questions—on trust, as it were.

It was done and, the Senate concurring, funds were made available to build the bomb that ended the war with Japan.

Typically, when it was suggested that he go to Oak Ridge, Tennessee, and see what was being constructed there, Rayburn snorted, "I don't want to go down there and look at all the pots and pans and bottles."

He was never a gadget-minded man. For many years he was faithful to the railroads for his travel between Washington and Texas. "I like to travel by train," he explained. "Takes two nights and a day to get home that way, and the best rest I ever get is during that time. I went up in a plane once, back in 1935. Made up my mind never to do it again." Finally, a few years before his death, he was converted to plane travel, largely through the efforts of Lyndon Johnson, who was jet-propelled long before planes were.

As the war began to turn in favor of the Allies, political unrest increased in the United States. People grumbled more and more about the economic controls, about rationing, about governmental bureaucracy, and nowhere was the grumbling louder than in Rayburn's own Texas. The Speaker rebuked the grumblers: "We still have among us that small minority who were afflicted with jaundice of the spine in 1940 and enlargement of the spleen in 1943." As for himself, he said regretfully, "I have no son to give to this war nor to the reconstruction of a stricken world after it is over, and I am wondering what real sacrifices I have made. I cannot think of a single one that hurts."

The Democrats were rent by intraparty bickering. Stormy threats to bolt the party on the issue of a fourth term for Roosevelt were loud in Texas. Rayburn himself was prominently mentioned as a nominee for Vice-President, but Texas sent two warring delegations to the convention and in the end the Speaker pledged his support to Harry S Truman.

In a speech before the Texas legislature, Rayburn made clear his own position regarding Roosevelt. "A greater Commander-in-Chief could not have been found if we had conducted a country-wide search for one," he said with staunch loyalty, "and as long as he is Commander-in-Chief and so long as he wants it, he shall have my uncomplaining support."

A member of that legislature, state senator G. C. Morris, who was a candidate against Rayburn in the 1944 Democratic primary, pitched his campaign entirely on the charge that Rayburn was a "yes-man" for the Administration. Rayburn had become a Washingtonian instead of a Bonhamite, Morris told the voters of the Fourth District, and had been an active participant in building a power-grabbing Federal bureaucracy. In fact, the war itself was only an excuse for keeping the bureaucracy in power and for continuing to expand it, Morris went on, promising that he would end the wartime controls and give the government back to the people.

Rayburn won handily enough, and in January of 1945 began his third full term as Speaker.

He was deeply worried about the state of the President's health. Even as he campaigned for the fourth term, he had felt that the President might not live to serve through the term. He was weighed with a sense of great personal sorrow as he contemplated a future without the man for whom he had fought so many savage legislative battles, the man to whom he had given an almost worshipful friendship. The patrician New Yorker and the country politician from Texas had come a long, hard way together.

When the news that Roosevelt had died reached Rayburn in his "Board of Education" room in the Capitol—the room from which Harry S Truman had been hastily summoned to the White House—the Speaker was shaken to the depths of his being. William S. White, a newsman who had known the Speaker for many years, wrote a moving description of the scene: "His heavy and immobile face was still in the shadows and the only movements upon it were the small and barely visible traces of tears. He swept them away roughly. For a long time no one said anything at all. Then Mr. Rayburn hunched his shoulders and, looking out unseeingly into the dusk, he spoke slowly in short, hard phrases as though talking to himself . . . an oath . . . that Sam Rayburn—Southern Democrat and all—had followed Franklin Roosevelt in life, and that Sam Rayburn would follow Franklin Roosevelt in death."

Then Rayburn himself went to the White House to pledge support to his old friend who had become the new President.

The relationship between Rayburn and Truman was exceedingly close. Both were practical politicians who detested sham and cant. They were plain-spoken men, men who expected loyalty because they gave it. They understood each other thoroughly.

In his first address to a joint session of Congress, Truman was so moved by the occasion that, as he related, he "forgot an important bit of protocol" and stood up to launch straightway into his speech.

155

"Mr. Speaker," he began.

He was immediately, although unobtrusively, interrupted by Rayburn, who was on the rostrum behind the President with Senator Kenneth McKellar of Tennessee, president pro tem of the Senate.

"Just a minute, Harry," the Speaker whispered, leaning toward the President. "Let me introduce you."

The microphone in front of Truman had already been turned on, and Rayburn's whisper was heard all over the House chamber and through the country over the radio network. So was his full-voiced introduction: "The President of the United States."

"I had now been introduced," Truman wrote in his *Memoirs,* "and so I went ahead."

Out of his experience, the Speaker gave some down-to-earth advice to the new President. "I have been watching the White House for many years," he told Truman. "I know some if its hazards. Your biggest danger is in the White House itself. Some of the people around you are going to try to do what they have tried to do to every President. They are going to try to build a fence around you, and in building that fence they will be keeping out the very people you should see. Don't let that happen."

Rayburn liked the way Truman took hold of his duties. "For a fellow whose first reaction was that he felt as if a ton of bricks had fallen on him, he learned mighty fast," the Speaker admiringly told mutual friends.

As a case in point he explained how the President, at his first meeting with congressional leaders, made clear his commitment to nonpartisanship on foreign affairs. One of the congressmen present mentioned the probable domestic political reaction to certain foreign relations proposals that the President had put forward. Truman gave the man a sharp stare, according to Rayburn, and said tartly, "Let's get one thing straight. I never want to hear that damn word 'politics' mentioned here again when we are discussing a thing like this."

The President, in turn, often expressed his appreciation of Rayburn's role. He realized that the Speaker faced a multitude of problems in dealing with the disparate membership of the House.

"The Speaker of the House knew what I was driving at," he wrote, "but with 435 congressmen on his hands he had to maneuver all the time to get what was necessary to carry on the government in all its functions. Every Speaker always gets interference from some fellow who wants to make a headline in his home-town newspaper. Now and then these moves may actually cripple the national welfare, but they may look good to the folks at home, where the situation may not be understood in its entirety."

Truman's admiration and personal fondness for Rayburn were matched by his respect for the speakership itself. He felt strongly that the presidential succession law should be changed to provide that only an elective official of the government could succeed to the highest elective office in the nation. Under a law enacted in 1896, the Secretary of State was next in line after the Vice-President, and other members of the Cabinet were to follow in order. This was wrong, Truman believed. Early in his Administration, he recommended legislation to place the Speaker of the House in succession after the Vice-President. Eventually a bill so providing was passed by Congress.

As the war came to an end, Rayburn did not share the fear generally expressed by economists that peace would bring a depression. Conceding that "it's a pretty tough deal to guarantee full employment for everyone," he did not fear that anything like the economic catastrophe of the thirties might lie ahead. "With all the billions of dollars people have saved and are now ready to spend," he thought, "they will be able to buy all the factories can make for years."

He had other worries, though, primarily worries of a political nature. With the end of the necessity for wartime unity, many Americans were showing increasing signs of restiveness and dissatisfaction. There was a great outcry to "bring the boys home!" from overseas. The controls that remained necessary in the period of transition from a war to a peace economy were bitterly assailed. All the people who had felt it expedient to keep their hate-Roosevelt and hate-Truman sentiments submerged, or at least largely submerged, during the war effort now surfaced their resentments.

Some Texans in high places and some leading Texas newspapers were especially vitriolic, and Rayburn bore the full brunt of their tirades. He had lived with the reality of a divided party for most of his political life. He was close to the problem, since he was that party's spokesman and also its titular head in Texas. The trouble in Texas dated as far back as the 1932 Democratic National Convention, when Rayburn had made himself the lasting target of the "Texas Regulars" by swinging the state delegation to Roosevelt after Garner had withdrawn. Ever since, Rayburn had been forced to battle the Lone Star anti-New-Dealers and anti-Fair-Dealers.

He was, of course, the old-fashioned kind of politician who places only his country above his party. A new congressman from Texas, a Republican, made the mistake on his first day in office of implying, in a statement to the press, that the Speaker did not put even his country first; Rayburn never forgave him for that. In general, however, he could condone, if not understand, Republicans: they were, for the most part, good men who were in the wrong party. But "Willkie-Democrats" or "Dewey-Democrats," or any other kind of hyphenated Democrats, were anathema to him. Everybody should stay with his own crowd, he believed and frequently said; *he* always stayed with his own crowd.

During the 1946 campaign, Rayburn was on the prowl throughout Texas and in other states as well. He had won his own renomination in the summer primary and was free to give his time to efforts to hold the House for the Democrats. It was a failing effort. This time the party lost both the House and the Senate.

Rayburn promptly issued a statement to the press: "I will not be the minority leader." He planned to go back to Washington as a plain member of the House.

However, two days after the election the Texas congressional delegation started a movement to draft him as floor leader. House Democrats from other states, unified in defeat as they rarely were in victory, joined in urging Rayburn to reconsider his decision. They made the final appeal he could not resist, that for the good of the Democratic party he must assume the leadership of the House minority.

His reluctant acceptance of the minority leader's post led, two years later, to the *Collier's Magazine* award for distinguished service to the Democratic party in 1947. The honor carried with it a cash grant of $10,000. Rayburn at once announced that he would use that money as a nucleus to establish a library in Fannin County. That was the beginning of the Sam Rayburn Library at Bonham.

In the Eightieth Congress, Joe Martin of Massachusetts was the new Speaker. He and Rayburn had been cronies for years, and the latter felt that if a Republican had to take over his job Martin was the best choice available.

"I predict for him a career such that history will record him as one of the great presiding officers," Rayburn told the House on the first day of the new session. "And I have the high privilege and great personal pleasure—if it has to come to that—of presenting the Speaker of the House of Representatives."

Rayburn had addressed the House only rarely while he was Speaker, but now that he was back down on the floor he plunged into the legislative fray with zest and skill. The word that "Mr. Rayburn is up" always filled the House chamber and the press gallery. Members and news reporters expected sound argument, presented succinctly and without bombast, from the stocky little Texan, and that is what they got.

There were some hard fights, and a good many were losing fights for Rayburn, in that Congress. As the minority leader, he led the battle against the Taft-Hartley labor bill, which the House nevertheless passed and then repassed over President

Truman's veto. Rayburn was successful, however, in getting some modification of provisions that he regarded as particularly unfair to labor. He fought also against the Republican-sponsored reductions in appropriations for the Department of Agriculture. Repeatedly he took the floor to defend some of the programs he had been instrumental in starting back in the thirties.

He had always regarded the Republican party as the chattel of "big business." He agreed with Truman: "Democrats work to help people who need help. That other party, they work to help people who don't need help." Now, to prove it further, Rayburn pointed to the majority's refusal to provide adequate funds for soil conservation, for rural electrification, for farm-to-market roads, and for school lunches. His feeling for the land as well as for the people of America was strong and personal.

"When I drive along the road or look out the train window and see the fertile soil of the country washed down to rock bottom and gutted with ditches," he said sadly, "it hurts me almost like the stick of a knife." He warned, "If we are the same kind of vandals for the next twenty-five years, even, that we have been in the past fifty years in the destruction of the fertility of our soil, we will not have any amount of surpluses to sell abroad, but we will be using every acre of this worn and torn land to raise the things that we have got to consume inside the United States of America."

At this stage in his political life, Rayburn no longer had any real reason to worry about whether the people of the Fourth District would keep him in Congress. He had become a permanent fixture so far as most of them were concerned. He continued to keep closely in touch with the district and to spend there all the time he could, for it was there that he liked to be. But his political concerns—since he was a national figure with national interests—were now diffused over the larger territory.

While the Eightieth Congress was wrangling, one of his well-to-do Texas friends engaged a public relations firm to conduct a public opinion poll in the Fourth District. The poll showed that Rayburn was in no trouble at all. The report did, however, quote candid comments from some individuals who were against him and against everything he advocated. Three copies of the report were made. One was retained by the public relations firm; the other two were given to the client, who sent a copy to his friend in Washington. As soon as he received it, Sam Rayburn telephoned his friend and ordered him to destroy the copy in his possession and to make certain that the other copy, too, was destroyed.

"What if word got out that I was having some of those polling fellers come in from outside to traipse around over my district?" he cried. "My folks wouldn't like it one bit and I wouldn't blame 'em. It's prying into their business. Tear up both copies!"

In the 1948 campaign, Rayburn and Truman went before the electorate determined to prove their contention that the Eightieth was a "do-nothing" Congress. It was the worst Congress he had ever served in, Rayburn charged, and he drew up a long list of indictments of the Republican majority. Indignantly, he cited their refusal to do anything to halt the postwar inflationary trend, their failure to pass minimum-wage legislation, their lack of action to correct the severe housing problem, and on and on.

Through the years, since the depression of the thirties, Rayburn had developed a set speech which he delivered with slight variations on nearly all political occasions and on many that were not political. Unless he had a written text, which he seldom did have, he was most likely, regardless of the announced subject, to veer off into a hard-hitting recital of the sins of the Republicans ("They're for the big boys every time") and the virtues of the Democrats ("The people know this is the party that belongs to them"). He used this speech often in the 1948 campaign.

He persuaded President Truman to come to Bonham "to meet the finest folks in the world." When several thousand people lined up in the highway in front of the Rayburn home,

prepared to file through the house and shake hands with the
President and his wife and daughter, the Secret Service men on
the scene became frantic. They said that under such conditions
it was impossible to guarantee the safety of the President.
Finally, they declared flatly that the reception could not go on.

"You can't do that," Rayburn protested. "These are my
friends. I'll stand here by the door and call them by name as
they come along and you will know they're safe."

So the reception proceeded. Rayburn greeted each of the
visitors by name, with rarely a slip-up, and passed them along
to the President.

The astounding Democratic victory in November kept Truman in the White House, gave the Democrats a majority of
263 to 171 Republicans in the House, and put Rayburn back
in the Speaker's chair. He settled down there comfortably to
take charge of the House of Representatives again.

"Rayburn runs the House out of his hip pocket," Senate
Majority Leader Lyndon Johnson used to say, sometimes in
admiration, sometimes in exasperation at what he considered
the Speaker's casual manner of operation.

It was true. Rayburn never had a large office staff nor did
he ever feel the need for one. Neither the Speaker's Room nor
his congressional office carried that air of purposeful urgency so
characteristic of Capitol Hill, where almost everybody constantly thinks of and works toward the next election. Rayburn
was apt to note his appointments on the back of an old en-
velope, which he then stuck into his pocket—indeed, his hip
pocket. If he was willing to wait his turn, anybody could get in
to see the Speaker. The reception room of his office was a leisurely place where visitors came and went, chatting amicably
or warily among themselves, placing telephone calls, reading
newspapers, altogether making themselves at home.

The man inside the private office, which was located only a
few yards from the Speaker's rostrum in the House chamber,
did his work restlessly but quickly. Interviews with him were
brief and to the point, with no time wasted. His numerous telephone conversations, whether with the President of the United

States or with a stranger, never lasted more than two or three minutes. The letters he dictated were unfailingly no more than a page in length and many consisted of only a few lines. In reply to a man who had written him a long letter one election year urging that he hold himself open for nomination as Vice-President, he answered with a single sentence: "Dear _____ : Please tell your friends I am not interested in being vice-president of anything."

Rayburn's relationship with the Washington press corps was on an equally relaxed basis. When he became Speaker he set up a regular schedule for seeing reporters in his office each weekday at 11:55 A.M., five minutes before the House session opened for the day. He also established a rule that everything he said was off the record unless he specifically stated otherwise, a rule directly contrary to that prevailing at the usual Washington news conference. He did this, he said, because he wanted to feel that he could speak freely about the legislative picture. "You'll have to go somewhere else to get your quotes," he told the reporters. He trusted them, with few exceptions, and they liked and respected him. A few became his close friends.

A Rayburn conference was not unlikely to end in laughter. At one, for example, a woman reporter asked, "What does the dignified Speaker of the House of Representatives think about these women tourists wearing shorts around the Capitol?" Rayburn looked at her quizzically. "Well, I haven't examined all of them," he said. "I wouldn't say that what women wear comes under the head of my business."

Rayburn never had a publicity man on his staff and rarely issued a written statement of any kind. He steadfastly refused to write the story of his life, with the help of no matter how gifted an editor, and rejected munificent offers from magazines and book publishers. "It's not worth the pain and agony," he declared. "Besides, I hate to see these books with all the 'I, I, I' stuff in them." He once complimented an associate by remarking, "He doesn't run around getting his name in the newspapers all the time."

His own name got into the papers, of course. Politics being

politics and newspapers being newspapers, the stories did not always portray him in glowing colors. A rather pompous acquaintance, having read such a story, spoke of it indignantly to Rayburn. "Why, I thought that was a pretty good article," the Speaker commented mildly.

"You did?" the man said in surprise. "For God's sake, why?"

"Well, it was more favorable than unfavorable," Rayburn replied. "I'll take a fifty-one per cent majority any time."

Such an attitude did much to account for his popularity with most reporters. Also, he could understand their problems. Paul Healy of the Washington bureau of the New York *Daily News* once was assigned by the *Saturday Evening Post* to do a profile of the Speaker. After considerable interviewing, Healy had his material well in hand and called in a photographer to get the pictures that must accompany the article. Because the picture-taking took longer than the subject considered necessary, Rayburn began to complain.

"Mr. Speaker, I have to get these pictures," Healy expostulated. "The *Post* will pay me fifteen hundred dollars for the article if I have the right pictures."

"Fifteen hundred dollars!" Rayburn repeated. "All right, Paul, we'll take whatever time you think we have to."

Rayburn's inborn kindliness was combined with a frontier instinct to aid people in times of distress. The morning after the daughter of a young Washington newsman died, the father answered the doorbell to find the Speaker of the House standing on his stoop. The reporter was surprised, for he knew Rayburn only from occasional attendance at his news conferences.

"I just came by to see what I could do to help," Rayburn explained. Nothing, the grieving father told him, all arrangements had been made. "Well, have you and your wife had your coffee this morning?" "No," said the reporter. "Well, I can at least make the coffee," Rayburn said, and proceeded to do so.

The reporter remembered that the Speaker had been scheduled to have breakfast at the White House that morning. He mentioned this.

"Well, I was," Rayburn admitted. "But I called the President and told him I had a friend who was in trouble and I couldn't come."

Rayburn's rapport with the newspaper people, like his success with members of the House, owed much to his universal reputation for candor and truthtelling. His word had the highest value of any political currency circulating in Washington. The President—any President—and other high government officials sometimes have difficulty in getting honest opinions because of the tendency of people to give the kind of advice they think is wanted. But not when they addressed Sam Rayburn. When he was asked for an opinion, he gave it straight from the shoulder. When he said he would do something, it was as good as done. As Roosevelt said, "The man's word is as binding as a legal contract."

A reporter once inquired of Rayburn how he could keep track without making notes of all the actions his position compelled him to tell people he would or would not take. "It's simple enough," answered Rayburn. "If you tell people the truth the first time, you don't have any trouble remembering what you said."

Old House members knew, and new members quickly learned, that they could depend absolutely on anything the Speaker told them. If he promised to try to get a Representative on a desired committee, the promise would be kept. If he gave his word that he would expedite legislation that would help a man in his district, quick House action on that bill was a certainty. Over the years, the Speaker made innumerable commitments and his reputation for fulfilling them was an important element in increasing the influence he commanded.

No less important an element in that influence was his reputation as a fair man in the Speaker's chair. Most Republicans and many Democrats differed with him on various political issues, but the House membership was virtually unanimous in acclaiming his fairness. He gave both sides on any legislative measure all the consideration to which they were entitled under the rules. He never had one of his rulings overturned by the House.

Remembering Champ Clark's consideration for him when he was a young congressman, and recognizing that he, too, might need help, Rayburn kept a watchful eye on incoming freshmen. He knew whether a new member was doing his committee work conscientiously, and knew whether he was taking a properly serious attitude toward his House duties. If the freshman measured up to these standards, he could banish any fear that he would be lost in the mass of the House membership. Rayburn was always on the lookout for new members who were worthy of advancement.

"It takes a while for a man to learn, and get established, and gain his full influence," the Speaker explained. "He doesn't reach his full usefulness in his first term or two. And the worst thing a district can do for itself, if it's got someone here doing the job right, is to keep changing its congressman. A man makes a record in the House the way he does in business or the law or anywhere else. It's hard work that makes the difference."

This concept of a Representative's job tied in closely with Rayburn's conviction that there was no adequate substitute for the seniority system. More often than not, he said, mediocre men did not stay in Congress long enough to advance to the chairmanship of a committee. Capable men were much more likely to stay. He added, "Those who are members of a committee for a long time learn the problems before the committee and become good leaders."

The helping hand he gave new members was of fundamental importance in Rayburn's masterful operation of the House. They appreciated and remembered his thoughtfulness and assistance. This bread cast upon the waters was returned over and over as the years went on.

Many House members who served with Rayburn later became members of the Senate, but he never regarded the move as a promotion. Publicly he was always properly respectful of "the other body," but in private he at times expressed contempt

for the pretensions of Senators. "I never had the slightest desire
to be a Senator or a Governor," he declared. "And I'd rather
be Speaker of the House than ten Senators."

Feeling as he did about the House, Rayburn experienced a
natural personal grief if a member did not behave as the
Speaker considered a Representative should behave. And he
could not abide any individual or collective action that made
the House appear foolish or put its members in a poor light.

Thus he found it in order to issue a formal prohibition
against the practice followed by some members of inserting
parenthetical indications of "applause" and "laughter" at appropriate points in speeches they had placed in the *Congressional Record,* although they had not delivered those speeches
on the House floor.

Thus he once burst out, after several members had taken
time to speak highly and at some length about a conductor of
the Boston Symphony Orchestra, "It costs eighty-five dollars a
page to print the *Congressional Record* in which these me-
morials are printed. The bill mounts up if we continue to
congratulate everybody in the United States. It's time to stop
issuing a memorial every time someone has done a grand deed
or lived a good life."

It was his sense of the dignity of the House that caused him
to refuse to allow the televising of committee hearings. His
position on the matter was unshakable. "When a man has to
run for re-election every two years," he explained, "the tempta-
tion to make headlines is strong enough without giving him a
chance to become an actor on television. The normal processes
toward good law are not even dramatic, let alone sensational
enough to be aired across the land."

His inflexibility on this question led to newspaper stories that
he disliked television because it was "newfangled." That was
nonsense. He liked television well enough and was especially
fond of watching baseball games and newscasts. He submitted
to television interviews from time to time and, as chairman of
three national conventions of the Democratic party, was a star

performer in his own right for a few days every four years.

Strong party man though he was, Rayburn was not an advocate of ironbound party discipline. He liked to say, "The House can work its will," and he was convinced that party caucuses on controversial issues were a waste of time and could do more harm than good by deepening the divisions between opposing factions. "I never was for blocs and never joined one," he recalled. "I wanted to be a free, independent legislator and vote my own sentiments." Naturally, he conceded, his sentiments on measures dividing Democrats and Republicans ordinarily would be with the former, "because I have had a part in making up their program."

The Speaker was often called on as a matter of course to help get jobs for deserving Democrats. Trying on one occasion to determine what could be done for a young Representative who had decided not to stand for re-election, Rayburn suggested that a Federal district judgeship might be the answer.

"Well, Mr. Speaker, I've never practiced law, you know," his friend explained. "I went directly from law school to the state legislature and from there to the House. I don't believe I am really qualified."

Rayburn stared at him in amazement, then broke into hearty laughter. "I've never heard that excuse before!" he said.

He was able to arrange to get his friend a different post.

Inevitably, some people took advantage of the Speaker in the name of friendship. A few lobbyists made a practice of hanging around the reception room of his office or trying to buttonhole him as he walked across the Speaker's lobby to the House chamber—merely to be seen in his company. For a friend he would write a letter of recommendation on a moment's notice. Sometimes, however, such letters were used for at least mildly questionable purposes. Rayburn was slow to become angered by such misuse unless, as he put it, he was "just plain stabbed in the back."

In one period of hue and cry over "influence peddling," a businessman was quoted in the press as having reported that a named lobbyist had boasted to him of being a long-time close friend of the Speaker. When reporters asked Rayburn about it, he reflected, then replied without emotion, "Well, if he said that, he's telling the truth. I have known him for a long time and we have always been friendly."

No scandal ever rubbed off on Rayburn. No one would have dared to approach this honest-faced man with a shady proposition.

That face became better known to the American people than the countenance of any Speaker. That was so not only because he held the speakership so long but also because he began to serve as permanent chairman of the Democratic National Convention about the time that television was beginning to exert a great influence on the people of the United States. In 1950 only 12 per cent of all American homes had television sets; but by 1960 88 per cent had them. Even in 1948 there had been television coverage of the convention. In 1952, and again in 1956, millions of Americans became familiar with the sight of the bald-headed man with the nearly grim face who, hunched behind a flag-bedecked rostrum, was able, somehow, to keep convention disorder from erupting into sheer chaos.

One of the most dramatic convention scenes in which he was a figure took place at Chicago in 1952 after the second ballot for the presidential nomination, on which Senator Estes Kefauver of Tennessee led Governor Adlai Stevenson of Illinois by thirty-eight votes. Rayburn recessed the convention—officially for dinner, actually to afford an opportunity for some vote-switching before the third ballot was taken. When the convention reassembled and the balloting began again, it became immediately obvious that switching had in fact taken place. Stevenson started to forge sharply ahead.

At this point, Senator Paul Douglas of Illinois, a strong Kefauver supporter, moved to usher his candidate toward the stage. The scene was one of turmoil and confusion as the two men approached and it became evident that Kefauver wished to address the convention.

Rayburn would not for a moment allow it. He knew that the Tennessean, realizing he no longer had a chance for the presidential nomination, proposed to withdraw and make a last desperate effort to be named as Stevenson's running mate. Chairman Rayburn would not interrupt the balloting. An expression of distaste twisting his mouth, he motioned the two Senators to seats on the platform. There they remained, angry and disconsolate, as the voting went on and Stevenson was chosen as the nominee.

Kefauver had made several mistakes. Even before the convention, his tactics had alienated the power structure in the Democratic party. At the convention, he had gone on television after the first ballot and declared, in white-faced rage, that he did not like the way the convention was being run, that Rayburn was handing down unfair decisions. Then he had committed the final error of appearing in the convention hall when he was still a candidate, which went counter to all of Rayburn's ideas of convention protocol. The convention's choice of Senator John Sparkman of Alabama as Stevenson's running mate met with the Speaker's approval.

Inevitably, Rayburn himself was talked of from time to time as a candidate for President. He took the talk with more than a grain of salt. He explained that he could not seriously aspire to the presidency because he was "born in the wrong part of the country at the wrong time." Prior to the 1952 convention the presidential rumors reached such a crescendo that he felt it necessary to issue a typically Rayburnesque statement. He said, "I have told my friends that I hoped they would not make a move in that direction, as I doubted that an effort along that line would be fruitful on account of matters that would take too long to go into."

In spite of this, Senator Richard B. Russell of Georgia, himself an active candidate for the nomination, told associates that Rayburn "has his lightning rod out a mile." But there was no evidence that Rayburn ever gave serious thought to pursuing the nomination. He was instinctively wary of the effect presidential ambitions have on a man. "Every good man in Washington who has been talked about for the presidency has been ruined by it," he told a friend. "Except," he added thoughtfully and with a half-smile, "me."

Rayburn campaigned hard for the Democratic ticket in 1952, but he was not optimistic about the probable outcome. The regular Democratic organization in Texas had deserted the party, and Rayburn had to set up his own campaign committee. Most of his efforts were devoted to holding his state for the Democrats. But he was not successful. Texas, too, went for General Dwight D. Eisenhower, the first time a Republican had carried the state since 1928.

In a post-election statement for the press, Rayburn, who had not even had an opponent, declared stoutly, "It took about 250,000 Republicans joined by bolters, so-called Democrats, to overthrow us." Privately, he told a man who had worked closely with him in the campaign, "We just got the *hell* beat out of us. It was the wrong time to hope to defeat a national hero." Rayburn was not given to deceiving himself.

A year later, after a Democratic victory in a California election, Rayburn hopefully wrote to a fellow Democrat: "I think we can sit awhile and watch them [the Republicans] try to do something, because we will have plenty of opportunity to criticize. They do not know where they are going on anything."

The Democrats did recapture both houses of Congress in 1954, but the 1956 presidential election was 1952 all over again, with the popular Eisenhower taking Texas along with most of the other states. Texans who were interested in such matters had the dazing experience in this year of hearing Sam Rayburn lustily booed at a Texas Democratic Convention—and booed not by Eisenhower Democrats but by self-styled liberals who thought the Speaker of the House had been too cooperative with the Republican President.

Rayburn took the booing grimly and went about his business, which, the Democrats having retained control of Congress, still was to run the House of Representatives as Speaker. On the other side of the Capitol, Lyndon Johnson was the majority leader and was doing a notable job of running the Senate.

Both Rayburn and Johnson were indeed cooperative in many respects with the Republican administration, for they were sympathetic with the problem of divided government which the President faced. But even during the two-year period when the Republicans controlled Congress, Rayburn spoke up critically when he felt criticism was in order.

Early in 1953, for example, reminding the House Republicans that their majority was a small one, the experienced old warrior voiced a tight-lipped warning: "I know how to cause trouble if I want to, for I know something about the rules of the House and the rights of the minority, and I want to see this Administration one of these days spread its wings and get off the ground, let us know where they are going, what they stand for, and when they are going to do something about what they do stand for."

At the end of that year's session he twitted his political opponents, "My Republican colleagues have my full sympathy because they return to face their constituents knowing that they have failed to keep their 1952 campaign pledges."

Rayburn was deeply incensed by the "twenty years of treason" charges leveled against the Democratic party by Senator Joe McCarthy and his loud followers. "Some of our backs are getting mighty sore," he told President Eisenhower. After the Democratic victory of 1954, Rayburn announced at once that the charges of treason must stop and would stop. He and Senator Lyndon Johnson also issued a statement assuring the President, and all American citizens, that they would continue to support a bipartisan foreign policy but would judge domestic issues entirely on the merits.

Rayburn often pointed out that he gave Eisenhower more frequent and more effective support than many members of the President's own party. He pointedly observed that "out of 164 votes in which his views prevailed during the past Congress, the President needed and received the margin of victory from the

Democrats on 121 votes." This was not the only time that the Speaker, party loyalist that he was, scolded the Republicans for their failure to support their own leader.

He liked Eisenhower as a person, spoke of him as "a good man," "a great general," "a great patriot," and said, "I think he wanted to serve his day and generation well." He took pleasure in reminding people that Eisenhower had been born in his own congressional district, at Denison, Texas, always adding jocularly, "He was a good *baby*."

He had expressed his reasoned judgment, however, back in 1948, when he was approached about the possibility of drafting Eisenhower as the Democratic candidate. "Good man," Rayburn had said then, "but wrong job."

Nevertheless, Eisenhower was the President and was President of all the American people, and so, as Rayburn said, Congress must work with him on matters affecting the welfare of the people. Sometimes this attitude caused the Speaker trouble with the politically obstreperous members of his own party, as in early 1955 when Congress had before it a resolution giving the President unlimited power to act in defense of Formosa against attacks by Communist China.

Rayburn believed the resolution to be unnecessary, holding that the President already had all the power he needed. Yet he told a delegation of House Democrats who called on him to protest passage of the resolution, "I want to show the world that we have a united country." The protesting Democrats expressed a dark suspicion that the resolution was no more than a scheme to make their party share the blame if the United States ran into trouble on Formosa. "Maybe so," Rayburn admitted, "but the country comes first. We are not going to play politics. I remember how the Republicans patted Truman on the back when he first went into Korea, then kicked him in the pants afterward. We're not going to do that."

The Speaker added that he wanted the resolution passed without divisive debate. It was passed quickly, with only one Democrat voting against it.

In the same year, Rayburn threw his strength behind an

Administration proposal to renew the Reciprocal Trade Act for three years instead of one year. The trade program had been an established policy of the government for some twenty years, but recently each renewal had been made only in the face of increasingly bitter controversy. This time the opposition to renewal, and especially renewal for a three-year period, was intense. Without Rayburn's influence, the bill unquestionably would have been defeated. However, as it was, the victory was won—by a one-vote margin, 193 to 192.

Again, in 1958, when threats of an economic recession caused some members of Congress to talk about reducing taxes in spite of an already heavily unbalanced budget, Rayburn upheld the Administration view that a tax cut would be unwise. Tax reduction legislation always has its political aspects, naturally, and signs of a race for political credit were becoming evident. It was at this point that Rayburn, Johnson, and Robert B. Anderson, Eisenhower's Secretary of the Treasury, worked out a gentlemen's agreement that there would be no surprise move by either the Administration or Congress. If a tax cut became clearly necessary to stimulate the economy, the requisite legislation would be handled on a cooperative basis, with political credit divided between Republicans and Democrats. Some of the Democrats continued to agitate for tax reduction, but the agreement held firm and Congress did not act in this area.

Cooperate though he did with Eisenhower, Rayburn nevertheless had a strong conviction that an ideal relationship was impossible between Speaker and President unless both were of the same party. "This doesn't mean they will always agree, of course," he explained. "But, generally speaking, they should have the same aims and the same ideas about the way to attain them."

Political partisanship and personal friendship were, however, two completely different matters, the Speaker believed, and had nothing to do with each other. He and his opposite number, Joe Martin, were extraordinarily close friends. An enthusiastic Democrat once asked Rayburn to go into Massachusetts and campaign for Martin's opponent. "Speak against Martin?" Rayburn said incredulously. "Hell, if I lived up there I'd vote for him."

He was greatly upset when Martin was deposed as House Republican leader at the beginning of the 1959 session of Congress. At a birthday reception for the Speaker on the evening of the day this occurred, Martin came in at a late hour. As he approached the receiving line, Rayburn stepped away from his host and hostess, Mr. and Mrs. Dale Miller, and with arms outstretched walked toward his friend. Tears came into Martin's eyes; Rayburn was equally affected.

"I won't have the minority leader's room any more, Sam," Martin said in a choking voice. "Can you find a little hideaway for me somewhere?"

"Joe," Rayburn said, "you can have any place in the Capitol you want."

Contemporary political observers often compared Henry Clay and Sam Rayburn as Speakers. Rayburn did not think much of the comparison. He admired Clay greatly, although he considered that the other had made a mistake in leaving the House for the Senate. But he thought that he and Clay worked in different fashions.

"I am not a compromiser," he contended. "I'd rather be known as a persuader. I try to compromise by getting people to think my way."

He was fully capable of making concessions when he had to do so to get needed votes, but he was not an easy man to sway once he had taken a position. He had been known to give voice to a mild and friendly complaint about then-Senator Johnson: "Lyndon listens to every fool that can grab him. Well, of course, he has to. I listen to them, too, but the difference between me and Lyndon is that he feels he has to answer them back. Usually, I just walk away."

Rayburn worried about Johnson, convinced the Senate leader, as he said, "took things too hard." He knew his friend was under constant pressure—but then, of course, he was, too.

"I have learned to go to bed and go to sleep without worrying," he said. "I figure that if I can't do my job standing up, there's no sense in stretching out and worrying about it all night."

The Speaker was so fond of Johnson that he often took particular pains to avoid upsetting the younger man. One day he telephoned an employee of the Senate majority leader and asked him to come over "for a visit." When he showed up, Rayburn came at once to the point.

"I guess Lyndon needs you over there," he said, "but he has a lot of other good men and I need you worse than he does. Would you like to come to work for me?"

The Johnson employee, flattered, said he would certainly like to think about it, adding that the idea held considerable appeal.

"How much money would you have to have?" asked the Speaker.

The other mentioned the salary he was getting and said that would be satisfactory. Rayburn professed ignorance as to whether the Speaker's office had a position open with such a salary. He called in John Holton, his administrative assistant for many years, and asked him. Yes, Holton said, such a position was open.

"Well, all right," said Rayburn, turning to the Johnson employee. "That suits me. Now—have you got the nerve to break it to Lyndon?"

"I'd rather not, to tell the truth."

Rayburn leaned back in his chair, throwing up both arms in a characteristic gesture. "I haven't got the nerve either," he admitted. "Guess we'll just have to forget it."

As he grew into an institution in his lifetime, Rayburn sometimes consciously, and with humor, enacted the role of a caricature of himself. Invited to address the New York Bond Club, he began his speech, "I accepted your invitation for two reasons. The first is that I wanted to see this many millionaires in one room. And the other reason is—" he paused and smiled, then put on the stern visage so familiar to television viewers of political conventions— "I just wanted to show you I'm not scared of you."

Set in his ways, he made a fetish of punctuality. He did not like to be late for an appointment, and he did not like it when people were late for appointments with him. One day he got off to a late start on the eighty-mile drive from Bonham to Dallas, where he was scheduled to address a medical convention. As it became evident that he would not be on time, he began to fume and mutter. Then he interrupted his fretting with a sudden laugh.

"I remind myself of a young farmer up in Fannin County who was going to get married at six o'clock on a Saturday afternoon," he explained to his driver. "He picked cotton till noon, and after dinner—they always have dinner at noon around Bonham—he shaved, took a leisurely bath, and finally was starting to get dressed. A friend burst in on him and warned him that if he didn't hurry he would be late to his own wedding. 'Well,' said the farmer, 'they cain't do no business till I git there.'"

The man who told this homely story, chuckling as he did, was the same man who could reach heights of unaccustomed and moving eloquence in speaking of the death of a friend like Alben Barkley. Barkley had come to the House of Representatives from Kentucky the year that Rayburn came in from Texas. They served together in the House until 1927. Thereafter, as Barkley went on to become a United States Senator, Senate majority leader, Vice-President, and then Senator again, the two men remained close friends. When Barkley died in 1956, Rayburn stood before the House he loved and, his voice rough with emotion, spoke his mind. "Out there somewhere, where the mighty spirits are gathered, the approach of Alben Barkley was received with open arms, because he was the equal of the mightiest spirits that assemble wherever that land or that clime may be. God bless his memory. God comfort his loved ones. God," said the Speaker, almost breaking down, "comfort me."

In 1960 Rayburn made a strenuous effort to bring about the nomination of Lyndon Johnson for President. But at that year's Democratic Convention—the first since 1948 over which Rayburn had not presided as permanent chairman—John F. Kennedy was nominated on the first ballot. When the nominee sought Johnson as his running mate, the Senator turned to his old friend and mentor for advice. Rayburn was at first firmly set against the idea. He relented only after Kennedy had come to him with a personal plea that Johnson was needed on the ticket for the good of the Democratic party. Once Rayburn had acceded to the proposal, Johnson accepted the vice-presidential nomination, thus fatefully moving into a position to become the thirty-sixth President after Kennedy's tragic death on November 22, 1963.

Although his eyesight was failing badly, Rayburn, a hale and vigorous seventy-eight, campaigned for the ticket and in triumph administered the oath of office to the new President, John Fitzgerald Kennedy, and the new Vice-President, Lyndon Baines Johnson, on January 21, 1961.

Late in life, the stocky Rayburn had become "Mr. Sam" to the entire nation. He had been so known for a long time in the Bonham area, where there was a large Rayburn family and where the neighbors identified the male members by calling them by their first names preceded by "Mr." The label "Mr. Sam" was brought to Washington by a young woman from Rayburn's district. She wrote a society column for a Washington newspaper in which she occasionally referred to "Mr. Sam," as she had heard the Speaker called back home. The appellation was taken up in the capital and from there carried across the nation by news writers, columnists, and radio and television commentators.

Patriarchal "Mr. Sam" to the nation, he was still "the man in charge" to the House of Representatives. It became apparent, however, in the first year of the Kennedy New Frontier that something would have to be done about the House Rules Committee. The committee consistently blocked action by the House on key Administration proposals; its conservative coalition of Democrats and Republicans simply refused to send the measures to the floor.

Many times in the past, Rayburn had been able to get bills out of the Rules Committee on the uncomplicated basis of personal friendship with the conservatives. By 1961, however, some of his old-time personal friends were gone. The coalition had become increasingly recalcitrant as the Kennedy social welfare measures were submitted.

So, in January of 1961, Rayburn reluctantly decided to move to change the political balance of the Rules Committee by enlarging its membership from twelve to fifteen. The addition of three members, if they were carefully chosen, could shift the balance of power on the committee from conservative to moderately liberal.

An intensely bitter fight followed. The opposition to the enlargement proposal was led by crusty Representative Howard Smith of Virginia, veteran chairman of the Rules Committee and a deep-dyed conservative. Smith and Rayburn had been good friends for a long time, but their friendship could not wholly withstand the rigors of this struggle. Smith received heavy Republican support in his opposition to the enlarging of his committee. In the end Rayburn won, but the outcome was close—217 to 212. It was a tremendous personal victory for the Speaker.

"We won," he said, his old face wreathed in smiles as he left the House floor after the vote, "and I am satisfied."

Even after the Rules Committee had been enlarged, Administration proposals continued to run into trouble in the House. It was a difficult session for Rayburn. Before it was over he was at his home in Texas. Sam Rayburn was ill.

He had been complaining of a backache before he left Washington on August 31. He thought, or at least said he thought, that he had lumbago. But on October 5 his illness was officially diagnosed as cancer. The whole country was deeply moved by this tragic news, for this was a man the country loved.

He died on November 18, 1961, in a Bonham hospital, and to the funeral service in the country church came most of the living great figures of the political world—including the current President, two past Presidents, and one future President: John F. Kennedy, Harry S Truman, Dwight D. Eisenhower, and Lyn-

179

don B. Johnson—along with friends and neighbors who had known "Mr. Sam" all their lives.

5

Of all the men who have served as Speaker of the House of Representatives, Sam Rayburn was closest to the people of the country. The people themselves recognized this closeness. The day of his funeral was in effect a national day of mourning as Americans everywhere crowded around their television sets to watch and listen to the simple service in the faraway Texas church.

The people of his Fourth Congressional District loved him best of all, of course. Also, they respected him, and regarded him ambivalently as a good neighbor, one of themselves, and as a "big man" in Washington. Much of what he did as Speaker, many of the affairs of global portent with which he was concerned, the folks at home did not understand at all!. They did know about such matters as good roads and rural electrification and easier credit for farmers. The rest they took on faith and friendship, and returned Mr. Sam to office election year after election year. So it came about that this rural Texas area, which dwindled in population from one census-taking period to the next and was down to 215,767 inhabitants in 1960, the last year it sent Rayburn to Congress, furnished the nation with a man who carried the common touch into councils with the movers and shakers of the world.

Rayburn gave as little thought as any man in public life ever had given to the impression he made on others. He never tried to project an "image." He was always supremely himself—and he had always known who he was. He was true all his life to his background, to his origins in a time and at a place that still bore the marks of the struggle for freedom and the harsh life of the frontier.

"He had no instinct for personal publicity, no flair for projecting to strangers the kind of man he really was," wrote his

180

friend, Hope Ridings Miller, after Rayburn's death. "Casual acquaintances often considered him just another conscientious public servant who lacked color and reached high rank through luck and seniority; a rather shy bachelor who side-stepped society so much because he felt out of place in it; an innately cautious politician with a mulish devotion to the Democratic party, and a sometimes cantankerous character who barked and balked at photographers."

So his friends and neighbors at home were not alone in failing to understand the man completely. Yet different people understood different segments of his whole being.

It was natural enough that he should be close to the people of the Fourth District of Texas. Yet he was no less admired and respected by the big-city politicians alongside whom he worked on many matters. It was he who would be sent, in the early days of the New Deal, to seek the vote of the volatile Fiorello LaGuardia of New York for measures on which some Republican support was essential. It was to his office that the politically sophisticated state and municipal bosses came for counsel on what their own people wanted and should have. It was Rayburn to whom representatives of the business community appealed for understanding of their problems.

In accordance with his nature, Rayburn spoke to all such diverse visitors in the same sparse language, with its almost Biblical simplicity. He had no capacity for smooth evasion, an art which is supposed to be a basic part of the successful politician's makeup. Those who wanted to know exactly where they stood with him could find out with no difficulty.

Rayburn was respected because he never went back on his word and because of his taken-for-granted honesty. He was honest even with himself, even against his own prejudices. Of the great uproar that followed President Truman's recall of General Douglas MacArthur during the Korean conflict, Rayburn said afterward, "I thoroughly endorsed his recalling Mac-Arthur. Sometimes people just get too big. Douglas MacArthur always felt like he was a man of destiny, I think. And," Rayburn

181

added, his honesty breaking out uncontrollably, "he just about was, to tell you the truth."

Mr. Sam was respected and was widely loved because he was a gentle, tolerant, kindly man, and because he accepted the outcome of political or legislative battles without gloating when he won, without resentment when he lost. He never held a grudge.

In addition to the respect and the affection that people felt for him was the admiration of the politically knowing ones for the Speaker's ability to get effective legislation out of the battling factions of the strife-torn Democratic party.

"He was always there when he was needed," said Lyndon Johnson. "His voice and judgment were heard and respected. In the end, it all added up to one thing—he did what was right."

His faith in the American people was absolute. "They have never failed to respond to the best interests of the country when this country was in danger and in a crisis," he said in an interview near the end of his life. "I have never doubted the patriotism or the willingness of the American people to sacrifice and to do the right thing."

Though he liked something about nearly everybody he knew and would listen to anybody who had anything worthwhile to say, he remained stubbornly convinced that his best source of knowledge and of ultimate wisdom was the plain people, "the everyday folks."

Once in the middle of a grinding campaign, when he was working from Democratic headquarters in Dallas, an assistant complained that half a dozen men were waiting to see him while Rayburn spent too much time with an old farmer.

"Listen," Rayburn growled in disgust, "I can learn more in ten minutes from that farmer than I can in two hours from one of your fat cats."

Harry Truman expressed a widely held opinion when he said, in presenting a hat to Rayburn at a luncheon, "Sam is the only man I know who could stay in Washington over forty years and still wear the same size hat he wore when he came here."

One of Rayburn's outstanding traits was optimism. He was

not one to long for "the good old days." He was convinced that Americans were living better, enjoyed better opportunities, and were better clothed, housed, fed, and educated in the middle years, and after, of the twentieth century than ever before. It was part of the harvest of his long life that this should be true, for he, the rural conservative, had played a major role in bringing about social reform through legislation.

As for the speakership itself, he carried out through many years the pledge he had made when he was first elected Speaker, a pledge to uphold "the prerogatives and powers of the House of Representatives." He restored the House to the position of eminence in the governmental structure from which many observers considered it had fallen in the preceding years. And he brought the speakership to a new high level of prestige and public respect.

Yet some thought he had made the House of Representatives too much of a one-man operation, so that there were dire results when he was no longer on hand to direct the operation. Representative Richard Bolling of Missouri said, two years after the Speaker had died, that Rayburn had "left the House in a shambles, institutionally." Bolling held that Rayburn had made what he called the institution of the House appear to work because he "had so much influence with individuals and had been around so long in a position of power." The House had ceased to work as an institution, the Missourian contended, after the Speaker's skilled hand had left the steering wheel.

Such criticisms of Rayburn were rare. Most of his friends—and Bolling himself was a friend and protégé of the Texan—were content to await the verdict of history on Sam Rayburn, the Speaker. Their memories were of Sam Rayburn, the man.

"Everyone who knew Sam Rayburn cherishes the moments they shared with him," Lyndon Johnson said, in a Jefferson-Jackson Day Dinner speech in 1962, "whether it was the hushed silence of the House before the tally of a vote is announced, during the unvarnished talk of the 'Board of Education,' amidst the hubbub of a Democratic convention, or a quiet walk around

Texas' old Fourth District to talk to the men and women of those flat black lands he loved so well."

The Rayburn his friends remembered was the man who, in an introspective mood with a group of intimates one evening, talked with fond reminiscence of Flag Springs, the little Texas community where, as a boy, he had gone to the one-room school.

"I am just a little way from Flag Springs," he said, adding, "You know, I just missed being a tenant farmer by a gnat's whisker."

To Sam Rayburn, any American was but a little way from some Flag Springs somewhere—and all the better for it, if he was not too proud to remember and not too selfish to help other people move up, too.

APPENDIX

First Congress

FREDERICK AUGUSTUS CONRAD MUHLENBERG (Federalist), born in Trappe, Pa., January 1, 1750; pursued an academic course; attended the University of Halle, Germany; studied theology and was ordained by the ministerium of Pennsylvania a minister of the Lutheran Church October 25, 1770; preached in Stouchsburg and Lebanon, Pa., 1770–74, and in New York City, 1774–76; when the British entered New York he felt obliged to leave, and returned to Trappe; moved to New Hanover, Pa., and was pastor of Lutheran congregations there and in Oley and New Goshenhoppen until August 1779; member of the Continental Congress, 1779–80; served in the state house of representatives, 1778–83, and was elected speaker November 3, 1780; delegate to and president of the state constitutional convention in 1787 called to ratify the Federal Constitution; elected to the First and the three succeeding Congresses (March 4, 1789, to March 3, 1797); served as Speaker during the First and Third Congresses; was not a candidate for renomination in 1796; president of the council of censors of Pennsylvania; appointed receiver-general of the Pennsylvania Land Office on January 8, 1800, and served until his death in Lancaster, Pa., June 5, 1801.

Second Congress

JONATHAN TRUMBULL (Federalist), born in Lebanon, Conn., March 26, 1740; was graduated from Harvard College in 1759; member of the colonial legislature of Connecticut, and served as speaker of the house; served in the Continental Army as paymaster, 1776–80; appointed secretary and first aide-de-camp to General Washington in 1780; elected as a Federalist to the First, Second, and Third Congresses (March 4, 1789, to March 3, 1795), serving as Speaker in the Second Congress; did not seek re-election, having become a candidate for Senator; elected to the U. S. Senate and served from March 4, 1795, to June 10, 1796, when he resigned; lieutenant governor of Connecticut from 1796 until the death of Governor Oliver Wolcott on December 1, 1797, when he became acting governor; was re-elected for eleven consecutive terms, and served as chief executive of the state from 1797 until his death in Lebanon, Conn., August 7, 1809.

Third Congress

FREDERICK A. C. MUHLENBERG. *See* First Congress

Fourth and Fifth Congresses

JONATHAN DAYTON (Federalist), born in Elizabethtown (now Elizabeth), N.J., October 16, 1760; was graduated from Princeton College in 1776; studied law; was admitted to the bar; during the Revolutionary War entered the Continental Navy as ensign in the Third New Jersey Regiment on February 7, 1776; promoted to regimental paymaster August 26, 1776; aide-de-camp to Major General John Sullivan, May 1, 1779; captain in the Third New Jersey Regiment March 30, 1780; was taken prisoner at Elizabethtown on October 5, 1780, and later exchanged; transferred to the Second New Jersey Regiment on January 1, 1781; honorably discharged November 3, 1783; member of the state general assembly, 1786–87 and 1790, and served as speaker in the last-named year; delegate to the Federal Constitutional Convention in 1787 and the youngest man to sign the Constitution; elected as a delegate to the Continental Congress to fill the vacancy caused by the declination of William Paterson, and was re-elected in 1788, thus serving from November 6, 1787, to March 3, 1789; served in the state council in 1790; elected as a Federalist to the Second and to the three succeeding Congresses (March 4, 1791, to March 3, 1799); served as Speaker during the Fourth and Fifth Congresses; was not a candidate for renomination in 1798, having become a candidate for the U. S. Senate; elected to the Senate and served from March 4, 1799, to March 3, 1805; was arrested in 1807 on the charge of conspiring with Aaron Burr on treasonable projects; gave bail and was subsequently released, but never brought to trial; died in Elizabethtown, October 9, 1824.

Sixth Congress

THEODORE SEDGWICK (Federalist), born in West Hartford, Conn., May 9, 1746; attended Yale College; studied theology and law; was admitted to the bar in 1766 and commenced practice in Great Barrington, Mass.; moved to Sheffield, Mass.; during the Revolutionary War served in the expedition against Canada in 1776; member of the state house of representatives, 1780 and 1782–83; served in the state senate, 1784–85; member of the Continental Congress, 1785–88; again a member of the state house of representatives, 1787–88, and served as speaker; delegate to the state convention that adopted the Federal Constitution in 1788; elected as a Federalist to the First and the three succeeding Congresses and served from March 4, 1789, until his resignation in June 1796; elected to the U. S. Senate to fill the vacancy caused by the resignation of Caleb Strong and served from June 11, 1796, to March 3, 1799; elected president pro tempore of the Senate June 27, 1798; elected to the Sixth Congress (March 4, 1799, to March 3, 1801) and served as Speaker; judge of the supreme court of Massachusetts, 1802–13; died in Boston, Mass., January 24, 1813.

Seventh, Eighth, and Ninth Congresses

NATHANIEL MACON (Democrat), born near Warrenton, Warren County, N.C., December 17, 1757; pursued classical studies and attended Princeton College; served in the Revolutionary War; member of the state senate, 1780–82 and 1784–85; moved to a plantation on the Roanoke River; elected as a Democrat to the Second and the twelve succeeding Congresses and served from March 4, 1791, until December 13, 1815, when he resigned, having been elected Senator; served as Speaker of the House, 1801–07; elected to the U. S. Senate on December 5, 1815, to fill the vacancy caused by the resignation of Francis Locke; re-elected in 1819 and 1825 and served from December 13, 1815, until his resignation on November 14, 1828; elected president pro tempore of the Senate May 20, 1826, January 2, 1827, and March 2, 1827; received twenty-four electoral votes for Vice-President in 1825; president of the state constitutional convention in 1835; presidential elector on the Democratic ticket of Van Buren and Johnson in 1836; died near Macon, Warren County, June 29, 1837.

Tenth and Eleventh Congresses

JOSEPH BRADLEY VARNUM (Democrat), born in Dracut, Middlesex County, Mass., January 29, 1750; completed preparatory studies; served in the Revolutionary army; member of the state house of representatives, 1780–84; served in the state senate, 1786–88 and 1795; commissioned colonel in the Seventh Regiment of Massachusetts Militia April 4, 1787, brigadier general November 22, 1802, and major general June 12, 1805; delegate to the state convention that ratified the Federal Constitution in 1788; justice of the court of common pleas; elected to the Fourth and the eight succeeding Congresses and served from March 4, 1795, to June 29, 1811, when he resigned, having been elected Senator; Speaker of the House during the Tenth and Eleventh Congresses; elected to the U. S. Senate in 1811 to fill the vacancy in the term commencing March 4, 1811, and served from June 29, 1811, to March 3, 1817; elected president pro tempore of the Senate December 6, 1813; delegate to the state constitutional convention in 1820; again a member of the state senate, 1817–21; died in Dracut, September 21, 1821.

Twelfth and Thirteenth Congresses

HENRY CLAY (Whig), was born in the district known as "the Slashes," Hanover County, Va., April 12, 1777; attended the public schools; studied law in Richmond, Va.; was admitted to the bar in 1797 and commenced practice in Lexington, Ky.; member of the state house of representatives in 1803; elected to the U. S. Senate to fill the vacancy caused by the resignation of John Adair and served from November 19, 1806, to March 3, 1807; again a member of the state house of representatives, 1808–09, and served as speaker the last year; elected to the U. S. Senate to fill the vacancy caused by the resignation of Buckner Thruston and served from January 4, 1810, to March 3, 1811; elected to the Twelfth and Thirteenth Congresses and served from March 4, 1811, to January 19, 1814, when he resigned; served as Speaker from November 4, 1811, until his resignation; appointed one of the commissioners to negotiate the treaty of peace with Great Britain in 1814; re-elected to the Fourteenth, Fifteenth, and Sixteenth Congresses (March 4, 1815, to March 3, 1821); elected Speaker on December 4, 1815, and served until October 28, 1820, when he resigned the office; elected to the Eighteenth and Nineteenth Congresses and served from March 3, 1823, to March 6, 1825, when he resigned; again served as Speaker from December 1, 1823, until the close of the Eighteenth Congress; appointed Secretary of State by President John Quincy Adams and served from March 7, 1825, to March 3, 1829; elected to the U. S. Senate on November 10, 1831, to fill the vacancy in the term commencing March 4, 1831; re-elected in 1836 and served until March 31, 1842, when he resigned; unsuccessful candidate on the Whig ticket for

President of the United States in 1824, 1832, and again in 1844; again elected to the Senate and served from March 4, 1849, until his death in Washington, D.C., June 29, 1852.

LANGDON CHEVES (Democrat), born September 17, 1776, in Bulltown Fort, near Rocky River, 96 District (now Abbeville County), S.C., where the settlers had taken refuge from the onslaught of the Cherokee Indians; received his early education at home and at Andrew Wood's School near Abbeville, S.C.; joined his father in Charleston, S.C., in 1786 and continued his schooling in that city; studied law; was admitted to the bar October 14, 1797, and commenced practice in Charleston; city alderman in 1802; member of the state house of representatives, 1802–10; presidential elector on the Madison ticket in 1808; elected attorney general of the state in 1808; elected as a Democrat to the Eleventh Congress to fill the vacancy caused by the resignation of Robert Marion, having previously been elected to the Twelfth Congress; re-elected to the Thirteenth Congress, thus serving from December 31, 1810, to March 3, 1815; succeeded Henry Clay as Speaker during the second session of the Thirteenth Congress; served as chairman of the Committee on Ways and Means and of the Naval Committee during the War of 1812; declined to be a candidate for re-election in 1814 to the Fourteenth Congress and also turned down the position of Secretary of the Treasury tendered by President Madison; resumed the practice of law; elected associate justice of law and appeal in December 1816; resigned in 1819; declined to accept a position as Associate Justice of the Supreme Court of the United States; elected president of the Bank of the United States March 6, 1819, and held this office until 1822, when he resigned; chief commissioner of claims under the Treaty of Ghent; resided in Philadelphia and Washington, 1819–26, and in Lancaster, Pa., 1826–29; returned to South Carolina in 1829; engaged extensively in the cultivation of rice in South Carolina and Georgia; tendered an appointment by the governor of South Carolina to the U. S. Senate to fill the vacancy caused by the death of John C. Calhoun, but declined; delegate to the Southern convention at Nashville, Tenn., in 1850 and to the state convention at Columbia, S.C., in 1852; died in Columbia, June 26, 1857.

Fourteenth, Fifteenth, and Sixteenth Congresses

HENRY CLAY. *See* Twelfth Congress.

JOHN W. TAYLOR (Democrat), born in Charlton, N.Y., March 26, 1784; received his early education at home; was graduated from Union College, Schenectady, N.Y., in 1803; studied law; was admitted to the bar in 1807 and commenced practice in Ballston Spa, N.Y.; organized the Ballston Center Academy; justice of the peace in 1808; member of the state assembly, 1812–13; elected as a Democrat to the Thirteenth and to the nine succeeding Congresses (March 4, 1813, to March 3, 1833); unsuccessful candidate for re-election in 1832 to the Twenty-third Congress; served as Speaker during the second session of the Sixteenth Congress and during the Nineteenth Congress; resumed the practice of law in Ballston Spa, N.Y.; member of the state senate, 1840–41; moved to Cleveland, Ohio, in 1843, and died there September 8, 1854.

Seventeenth Congress

PHILIP PENDLETON BARBOUR (Democrat), born at "Frascati," near Gordonsville, Orange County, Va., May 25, 1783; attended common and private schools; was graduated from William and Mary College, Williamsburg, Va., May 25, 1799; studied law; was admitted to the bar in 1800 and commenced practice in Bardstown, Ky.; returned to Virginia in 1801 and practiced law in Gordonsville; member of the state house of delegates, 1812–14; elected as a Democrat to the Thirteenth Congress to fill a vacancy caused by the death of John Dawson; re-elected to the Fourteenth and to the four succeeding Congresses, thus serving from September 19, 1814, to March 3, 1825; was not a candidate for renomination in 1824; served as Speaker of the House in the Seventeenth Congress; offered the professorship of law in the University of Virginia in 1825, but declined; appointed a judge of the general court of Virginia and served for two years, resigning in 1827; elected to the Twentieth and Twenty-first Congresses and served from March 4, 1827, until his resignation on October 15, 1830; president of the Virginia constitutional convention in 1829; appointed by President Jackson, June 1, 1830, judge of the United States Circuit Court for the Eastern District of Virginia, declining the chancellorship and the post of attorney general; refused nominations for judge of the court of appeals, for governor, and for U. S. Senator; appointed Associate Justice of the United States Supreme Court and served from March 15, 1836, until his death in Washington, D.C., February 25, 1841.

Eighteenth Congress

HENRY CLAY. *See* Twelfth Congress

Nineteenth Congress

JOHN W. TAYLOR. *See* Sixteenth Congress

Twentieth, Twenty–first, Twenty–second and Twenty–third Congresses

ANDREW STEVENSON (Democrat), born in Culpeper County, Va., January 21, 1784; pursued classical studies; attended William and Mary College, Williamsburg, Va.; studied law; was admitted to the bar and commenced practice at Richmond, Va.; member of the state house of delegates, 1809–16 and 1818–21, and served as Speaker, 1812–15; unsuccessful candidate in 1814 and 1816 for election to Congress; elected as a Democrat to the Seventeenth and to the six succeeding Congresses and served from March 4, 1821, until his resignation, because of ill health, June 2, 1834; served as Speaker of the House, 1827–34; Minister to Great Britain, 1836–41; engaged in agricultural pursuits in Albermarle County, Va.; in 1845 was elected a member of the Board of Visitors of the University of Virginia at Charlottesville, and in 1856 was elected rector; died at his home in Albermarle County, January 25, 1857.

JOHN BELL (Whig), born near Nashville, Tenn., February 15, 1797; was graduated from the University of Nashville in 1814; studied law; was admitted to the bar in 1816 and commenced practice in Franklin, Tenn.; served in the state senate in 1817; declined to be a candidate for re-election and moved to Nashville; elected as a Democrat to the Twentieth and as a Whig to the Twenty-first and to the five succeeding Congresses (March 4, 1827, to March 3, 1841); Speaker of the House during the second session of the Twenty-third Congress in 1834; appointed by President Harrison as Secretary of War, March 5, 1841, and served until September 12, 1841, when he resigned; member of the state house of representatives in 1847; elected as a Whig to the U. S. Senate in 1847; re-elected in 1853, thus serving from November 22, 1847, to March 3, 1859; unsuccessful candidate for President of the United States on the Constitutional Union ticket in 1860; died at his home near Cumberland Furnace, Tenn., September 10, 1869.

Twenty–fourth and Twenty–fifth Congresses

JAMES KNOX POLK (Democrat), born in Mecklenburg County, N.C., November 2, 1795; moved to Tennessee in 1806 with his parents, who settled in what later became Maury County; attended the common schools and was tutored privately; was graduated from the University of North Carolina at Chapel Hill in 1818; studied law; was admitted to the bar in 1820 and commenced practice in Columbia, Tenn.; chief clerk of the state senate, 1821–23; elected as a Democrat to the Nineteenth and to the six succeeding Congresses (March 4, 1825, to March 3, 1839); did not seek renomination in 1838, having become a candidate for governor; served as Speaker during the sessions of the Twenty-fourth and Twenty-fifth Congresses; governor of Tennessee, 1839–41; elected President of the United States in 1844 on the Democratic ticket; was inaugurated on March 4, 1845, and served until March 3, 1849; declined to be a candidate for renomination; died in Nashville, Tenn., June 15, 1849.

Twenty–sixth Congress

ROBERT MERCER TALIAFERRO HUNTER (Democrat), born near Loretto, Essex County, Va., April 21, 1809; tutored at home; was graduated from the University of Virginia at Charlottesville; studied law; was admitted to the bar in 1830 and commenced practice at Lloyds, Va.; member of the state house of delegates in 1833; served in the state senate, 1835–37; elected as a Democrat to the Twenty-fifth and to the two succeeding Congresses (March 4, 1837, to March 3, 1843); unsuccessful candidate for re-election to the Twenty-eighth Congress; elected to the Twenty-ninth Congress (March 4, 1845, to March 3, 1847); served as Speaker of the House in the Twenty-sixth Congress; elected to the U. S. Senate and served from March 4, 1847, to March 28, 1861, when he withdrew; author of the tariff act of 1857; candidate for the presidential nomination in 1860; declined the position of Secretary of State tendered him by Presidents Pierce and Buchanan; delegate from Virginia to the Confederate Provincial Congress at Richmond; Confederate Secretary of State from July 25, 1861, to February 18, 1862; served in the Confederate Senate from Virginia in the First and Second Congresses, 1862–65, and was president pro tempore on various occasions; was one of the peace commissioners that met with President Lincoln and his party in Hampton Roads in February 1865; elected state treasurer of Virginia in 1877; collector at Tappahannock, Va., in 1885; died near Lloyds, July 18, 1887.

Twenty–seventh Congress

JOHN WHITE (Whig), born near Cumberland Gap (now Middlesboro), Ky., February 14, 1802; received a limited schooling; studied law and was admitted to the bar; commenced practice in Richmond, Ky.; member of the state house of representatives in 1832; elected as a Whig to the Twenty-fourth and to the four succeeding Congresses (March 4, 1835, to March 3, 1845); served as Speaker of the House in the Twenty-seventh Congress; appointed judge of the nineteenth judicial district of Kentucky and served from February 8, 1845, until his death in Richmond, Ky., September 22, 1845.

Twenty–eighth Congress

JOHN WINSTON JONES (Democrat), born near Amelia Court House, Amelia County, Va., November 22, 1791; attended private schools; was graduated from the law department of William and Mary College, Williamsburg, Va., in 1813; was admitted to the bar the same year and commenced practice in Chesterfield County, Va.; prosecuting attorney for the fifth Virginia circuit in 1818; member of the state constitutional convention, 1829–30; elected as a Democrat to the Twenty-fourth and to the four succeeding Congresses (March 4, 1835, to March 3, 1845); served as Speaker of the House in the Twenty-eighth Congress; declined to be a candidate for renomination in 1844; resumed the practice of law and also engaged in agricultural pursuits; member of the state house of delegates in 1846 and served as speaker; re-elected in 1847 but resigned because of ill health; died at his home in Chesterfield County, January 29, 1848.

Twenty–ninth Congress

JOHN WESLEY DAVIS (Democrat), born in New Holland, Lancaster County, Pa., April 16, 1799; moved to Cumberland

County, Pa., with his parents, who settled near Shippensburg; completed preparatory studies; studied medicine; was graduated from the Baltimore Medical College in 1821; moved to Carlisle, Ind., in 1823 and practiced medicine; surrogate of Sullivan County, 1829–31; member of the state house of representatives, 1831–33, and served as speaker in 1831; commissioner to negotiate an Indian treaty in 1834; elected as a Democrat to the Twenty-fourth Congress (March 4, 1835, to March 3, 1837); declined to be a candidate for renomination in 1836 because of ill health; elected to the Twenty-sixth Congress (March 4, 1839, to March 3, 1841); unsuccessful candidate for re-election in 1840; again a member of the state house of representatives, 1841–43, and served as speaker in 1841; elected to the Twenty-eighth and Twenty-ninth Congresses (March 4, 1843, to March 3, 1847); served as Speaker of the House in the Twenty-ninth Congress; was not a candidate for renomination in 1846; appointed by President Polk United States Commissioner to China and served from 1848 to 1851, when his successor was appointed; member of the state house of representatives, 1851–52 and 1857; delegate to the Democratic National Convention at Baltimore in 1852 which nominated Pierce and King, and served as president of the convention; appointed by President Pierce as governor of Oregon Territory and served in 1853 and 1854; member of the Board of Visitors to the U.S. Military Academy at West Point in 1858; died in Carlisle, Sullivan County, Ind., August 22, 1859.

Thirtieth and Thirty-first Congresses

ROBERT CHARLES WINTHROP (Whig), born in Boston, Mass., May 12, 1809; attended Roxbury High School, and was graduated from Harvard University in 1828; studied law with Daniel Webster; was admitted to the bar in 1831 and practiced in Boston; member of the state house of representatives, 1835–40, and served as speaker, 1838–40; elected as a Whig to the Twenty-sixth Congress to fill the vacancy caused by the resignation of Abbott Lawrence; re-elected to the Twenty-seventh Congress, thus serving from November 9, 1840, to May 25, 1842, when he resigned; subsequently elected to the Twenty-seventh Congress to fill the vacancy caused by the resignation of his successor; re-elected to the Twenty-eighth and to the three succeeding Congresses, thus serving from November 29, 1842, to July 30, 1850, when he again resigned to become Senator; was Speaker of the House during the Thirtieth Congress and a portion of the Thirty-first Congress; appointed to the U.S. Senate on July 27, 1850, to fill the vacancy caused by the resignation of Daniel Webster and served from July 30, 1850, to February 1, 1851, when a successor was elected; unsuccessful candidate for the vacancy in 1851; was an unsuccessful candidate for governor of Massachusetts the same year; was presidential elector on the Whig ticket of Scott and Graham in 1852; engaged in literary, historical, and philanthropic pursuits; died in Boston, Mass., November 16, 1894.

HOWELL COBB (Democrat), born in Jefferson Co., Ga., September 7, 1815; moved with his father to Athens, Ga., in childhood; was graduated from Franklin College (then a part of the University of Georgia) at Athens in 1834; studied law; was admitted to the bar and commenced practice at Athens in 1836; presidential elector on the Van Buren and Johnson ticket in 1836; solicitor-general of the western judicial circuit of Georgia, 1837–41; elected as a Democrat to the Twenty-eighth and to the three succeeding Congresses (March 4, 1843, to March 3, 1851); served as Speaker of the House in the Thirty-first Congress; governor of Georgia, 1851–53; elected to the Thirty-fourth Congress (March 4, 1855, to March 3, 1857); Secretary of the Treasury in the Cabinet of President Buchanan and served from March 6, 1857, to December 10, 1860, when he resigned; chairman of the convention of delegates from the seceded states which assembled in Montgomery, Ala., February 24, 1861, to form a Confederate government; during the Civil War was appointed a brigadier general in the Confederate Army February 13, 1862, and promoted to major general September 9, 1863; surrendered at Macon, Ga., April 20, 1864; died in New York City, October 9, 1868.

Thirty–second and Thirty–third Congresses

LINN BOYD (Democrat), born in Nashville, Tenn., November 22, 1800; pursued preparatory studies; moved with his parents to New Design, Trigg County, Ky.; engaged in agricultural projects in Calloway County; member of the state house of representatives, 1827–32; returned to Trigg County in 1834; elected as a Democrat to the Twenty-fourth Congress (March 4, 1835, to March 3, 1837); unsuccessful candidate for re-election in 1836 to the Twenty-fifth Congress; elected to the Twenty-sixth and to the seven succeeding Congresses (March 4, 1839, to March 3, 1855); served as Speaker of the House in the Thirty-second and Thirty-third Congresses; moved to Paducah, Ky., in 1852; elected lieutenant governor of Kentucky in 1859, but when the senate convened was too ill to preside over its deliberations; died in Paducah, December 17, 1859.

Thirty–fourth Congress

NATHANIEL PRENTICE BANKS (American Party), born in Waltham, Mass., January 30, 1816; attended the common schools; a machinist by trade; editor of a weekly paper in Waltham; clerk in the customhouse in Boston; studied law; was admitted to the Suffolk County bar and commenced practice in Boston; member of the state house of representatives, 1849–52, for two years serving as speaker; member of the state constitutional convention of 1853; elected as a Coalition Democrat to the Thirty-third Congress and as the candidate of the American Party to the Thirty-fourth Congress, of which he was chosen Speaker; elected as a Republican to the Thirty-fifth Congress, thus serving from March 4, 1853, until he resigned December 24, 1857, to become governor; governor of Massachusetts from

January 1858 until January 1861; moved to Chicago; vice-president of the Illinois Central Railroad; entered the Union Army as a major general of Volunteers, May 16, 1861; received the thanks of Congress January 18, 1864, "for the skill, courage, and endurance which compelled the surrender of Port Hudson, and thus removed the last obstruction to the free navigation of the Mississippi River"; honorably mustered out August 24, 1865; returned to Massachusetts; elected as a Union Republican to the Thirty-ninth Congress to fill a vacancy caused by death; re-elected as a Republican to the Fortieth and to the two succeeding Congresses, thus serving from December 4, 1865, to March 3, 1873; unsuccessful Liberal and Democratic candidate for re-election in 1872 to the Forty-third Congress; appointed United States Marshal on March 11, 1879; served until April 23, 1888; elected as a Republican to the Fifty-first Congress (March 4, 1889, to March 3, 1891); unsuccessful candidate for renomination in 1890 to the Fifty-second Congress; died in Waltham, September 1, 1894.

Thirty–fifth Congress

JAMES LAWRENCE ORR (Democrat), born in Craytonville, Anderson County, S.C., May 12, 1822; attended the public schools and was graduated from the University of Virginia in 1842; studied law; was admitted to the bar and commenced practice in Anderson, S.C., in 1843; engaged in newspaper work; member of the state house of representatives, 1842–48; elected as a Democrat to the Thirty-first and to the four succeeding Congresses (March 4, 1849, to March 3, 1859); Speaker of the House in the Thirty-fifth Congress; was not a candidate for renomination in 1858; resumed the practice of law at Craytonville; member of the southern rights convention held in Charleston, S.C., in 1851; delegate to the Democratic National Convention in Charleston in 1860; member of the secession convention in 1860; one of three commissioners sent to Washington, D.C., to treat with the Federal government for the surrender of forts in Charleston Harbor; member of the Confederate Senate in 1861; served in the Confederate Army during the Civil War; special commissioner sent to President Johnson to negotiate the establishment of provisional government for the state of South Carolina in 1865; member of the state constitutional convention in 1865; elected governor of South Carolina as a Republican in 1866; president of the state convention held at Columbia in July 1868; delegate to the Union National Convention at Philadelphia in August 1866; judge of the eighth judicial circuit, 1868–70; member of the Republican state convention at Columbia in August 1872; delegate to the Republican National Convention at Philadelphia in 1872; appointed by President Grant as Minister to Russia in December 1872; died in St. Petersburg, Russia, May 5, 1873.

Thirty–sixth Congress

WILLIAM PENNINGTON (Whig), born in Newark, N.J., May 4, 1796; completed preparatory studies; was graduated from Princeton College in 1813; clerk of the United States district court, 1815–26; studied law; was admitted to the bar and commenced practice in Newark in 1820; member of the state general assembly in 1828 and served as sergeant of law in 1834; governor of New Jersey from 1837 to 1843; appointed governor of Minnesota Territory by President Fillmore but declined to accept; elected as a Whig to the Thirty-sixth Congress (March 4, 1859, to March 3, 1861) and served as Speaker; unsuccessful Republican candidate for re-election in 1860 to the Thirty-seventh Congress; died in Newark, N.J., February 16, 1862.

Thirty–seventh Congress

GALUSHA AARON GROW (Republican), born in Ashford (now Eastford), Windham County, Conn. August 31, 1823; moved to Glenwood, Susquehanna County, Pa., in May 1834;

attended the common schools and Franklin Academy, Susque-hanna County; was graduated from Amherst College, Amherst, Mass., in 1844; studied law; was admitted to the bar of Sus-quehanna County in 1847 and practiced; elected as a Free-Soil Democrat to the Thirty-second, Thirty-third, and Thirty-fourth Congresses and as a Republican to the Thirty-fifth and to the two succeeding Congresses (March 4, 1851, to March 3, 1863); unsuccessful Republican nominee for Speaker in 1857; served as Speaker in the Thirty-seventh Congress; delegate to the Re-publican National Conventions in 1864, 1884, and 1892; presi-dent of the Houston & Great Northern Railroad Co. of Texas, 1871–76; returned to Pensylvania and engaged in lumber, oil, and soft-coal business; elected to the Fifty-third Congress to fill a vacancy caused by death; re-elected to the Fifty-fourth and to the three succeeding Congresses, thus serving from February 25, 1894, to March 3, 1903; declined a renomination in 1902; died in Glenwood, near Scranton, Pa., March 31, 1907.

Thirty–eighth, Thirty–ninth, and Fortieth Congresses

SCHUYLER COLFAX (Republican), born in New York City March 23, 1823; attended the common schools; in 1836 moved with his parents to New Carlisle, Ind., where he was appointed deputy auditor of St. Joseph County in 1841 by his stepfather, with office in South Bend; became a legislative correspondent in Indianapolis; purchased an interest in the South Bend *Free Press* and changed its name in 1845 to the *St. Joseph Valley Register,* the Whig organ of northern Indiana; delegate to the Whig National Conventions in 1848 and 1852; member of the state constitutional convention in 1850; unsuccessful Whig can-didate for election to the Thirty-second Congress; elected as a Republican to the Thirty-fourth and to the six succeeding Congresses (March 4, 1855, to March 3, 1869); was not a can-didate for renomination in 1868, having become the Repub-lican candidate for Vice-President; served as Speaker of the House in the Thirty-eighth, Thirty-ninth, and Fortieth Congresses; elected Vice-President on the Republican ticket headed by General Ulysses S. Grant in 1868, was inaugurated March 4, 1869, and served until March 3, 1873; unsuccessful candidate for renomination in 1872; declined the chief editorship of the New York *Tribune* the same year; exonerated from charges of corruption brought against members of Congress in 1873 in connection with the Crédit Mobilier of America; devoted his time to lecturing; died in Mankato, Blue Earth County, Minn., January 13, 1885.

THEODORE MEDAD POMEROY (Republican), born in Cayuga, N.Y., December 31, 1824; attended the common schools and Munroe Collegiate Institute, Ellridge, N.Y.; was graduated from Hamilton College, Clinton, N.Y., in 1842; studied law; was admitted to the bar in 1846 and commenced practice in Auburn, N.Y.; district attorney of Cayuga County, 1850–56; member of the state assembly in 1857; delegate to the Republican National Convention in 1860 and 1876, and served as temporary chairman of the latter convention; elected as a Republican to the Thirty-seventh and to the three succeeding Congresses (March 4, 1861, to March 3, 1869); declined to be a candidate for renomination in 1868; during the Fortieth Congress was elected Speaker of the House on the last day of session, March 3, 1869, serving one day only, after Colfax had resigned to be inaugurated Vice-President; first vice-president and general counsel of the American Express Co. in 1868; engaged in banking in Auburn after 1870; mayor of Auburn, 1875–76; died in that city March 23, 1905

Forty–first, Forty–second, and Forty–third Congresses

JAMES GILLESPIE BLAINE (Republican), born in West Brownsville, Washington County, Pa., January 31, 1830; was graduated from Washington College, Washington, Pa., in 1847; was for a time teacher in the Western Military Institute, Blue Lick Springs, Ky.; returned to Pennsylvania; studied law;

taught advanced subjects in the Pennsylvania Institution for the Blind at Philadelphia, 1852–54; moved in 1854 to Maine, where he edited the Portland *Advertiser* and the Kennebec *Journal*; member of the state house of representatives, 1858–62, serving the last two years as speaker; elected as a Republican to the Thirty-eighth and to the six succeeding Congresses and served from March 4, 1863, to July 10, 1876, when he resigned; served in the Forty-first, Forty-second, and Forty-third Congresses as Speaker of the House; was a leading candidate for the nomination for President on the Republican ticket in 1876 and 1880; appointed and subsequently elected to the U.S. Senate to fill a vacancy caused by resignation; re-elected and served from July 10, 1876, to March 5, 1881, when he resigned to become Secretary of State in the Cabinet of President Garfield; Secretary of State from March 5 to December 12, 1881; unsuccessful Republican candidate for President in 1884; Secretary of State in the Cabinet of President Benjamin Harrison and served from March 7, 1889, to June 4, 1892, when he resigned; aided in organizing and was the first president of the Pan American Congress; died in Washington, D.C., January 27, 1893.

Forty–fourth Congress

MICHAEL CRAWFORD KERR (Democrat), born in Titusville, Crawford County, Pa., March 15, 1827; attended the common schools and Erie Academy; was graduated from the law department of Louisville (Ky.) University in 1851; was admitted to the bar and commenced practice in New Albany, Ind., in 1852; city attorney in 1854; prosecuting attorney of Floyd County in 1855; member of the state house of representatives, 1856–57; reporter of the supreme court of Indiana, 1862–65; elected as a Democrat to the Thirty-ninth and to the three succeeding Congresses (March 4, 1865, to March 3, 1873); unsuccessful candidate for re-election in 1872 to the Forty-third Congress; elected to the Forty-fourth Congress and served from

March 4, 1875, until his death; elected Speaker of the House
for the Forty-fourth Congress on December 6, 1875, and served
until his death; died at Rockbridge Alum Springs, Rockbridge
County, Va., August 19, 1876.

SAMUEL JACKSON RANDALL (Democrat), born in Philadelphia, Pa., October 10, 1828; attended the common schools
and the University Academy in Philadelphia; engaged in mer-
cantile pursuits; member of the common council of Philadelphia, 1852–55; member of the state senate, 1858–59; during the
Civil War served as a member of the First Troop of Philadelphia in 1861 and was in the Union Army three months of that
year and again in 1863; was promoted to provost marshal at
Gettysburg; elected to the Thirty-eighth and to the thirteen succeeding Congresses and served from March 4, 1863, until his
death; Speaker of the House during the last session of the Forty-
fourth and also during the Forty-fifth and Forty-sixth Congresses; died in Washington, D.C., April 13, 1890.

Forty–fifth and Forty–sixth Congresses

SAMUEL J. RANDALL. *See Forty-fourth Congress*

Forty–seventh Congress

JOSEPH WARREN KEIFER (Republican), born near Springfield, Bethel Township, Clark County, Ohio, January 30, 1836;
attended the common schools and Antioch College, Yellow
Springs, Ohio; studied law; was admitted to the bar and commenced practice in Springfield, Ohio, January 12, 1858; during
the Civil War enlisted in the Union Army on April 19, 1861;
commissioned major in the Third Ohio Volunteer Infantry
April 27, 1861; lieutenant colonel February 12, 1862; colonel
of the One Hundred and Tenth Ohio Volunteer Infantry September 30, 1862; brevetted brigadier general of Volunteers
October 19, 1864; severely wounded in the Battle of the Wilder-

ness May 5, 1864; promoted to major general April 9, 1865; mustered out June 27, 1865; resumed the practice of law in July 1865; member Ohio state senate, 1868–69; elected as a Republican to the Forty-fifth and to the three succeeding Congresses (March 4, 1877, to March 3, 1885); served as Speaker of the House in the Forty-seventh Congress; unsuccessful candidate for renomination in 1884; major general of Volunteers in the Spanish-American War from June 9, 1898, to May 12, 1899; first commander-in-chief of the Spanish War Veterans in 1900 and 1901; elected to the Fifty-ninth and to the two succeeding Congresses (March 4, 1905, to March 3, 1911); unsuccessful candidate for re-election in 1910; addressed the Conference on Universal Peace in Brussels in 1911 and was in Berlin, Germany, in 1914, on his way to Stockholm to address the conference of that year, when the First World War began; resumed his law practice; president of the Lagonda National Bank of Springfield, Ohio, for more than fifty years; died in Springfield, April 22, 1932.

Forty–eighth, Forty–ninth, and Fiftieth Congresses

JOHN GRIFFIN CARLISLE (Democrat), born in Campbell (now Kenton) County, Ky., September 5, 1835; attended the common schools; taught school in Covington and elsewhere for five years; studied law; was admitted to the bar in March 1858 and commenced practice in Covington; member of the state house of representatives, 1859–61; nominated for presidential elector on the Democratic ticket in 1864, but declined to run; member of the state senate in 1866, re-elected in August 1869 and resigned in 1871; delegate at large to the Democratic National Convention at New York City in 1868; lieutenant governor of Kentucky, serving from August 1871 to September 1875; was editor of the Louisville *Daily Ledger* in 1872; alternate presidential elector at large in 1876; elected as a Democrat to the Forty-fifth and to the six succeeding Congresses and served from March 4, 1877, to May 26, 1890, when he resigned, having been elected Senator; served as Speaker of the House in the Forty-eighth, Forty-ninth, and Fiftieth Congresses; elected to the U.S. Senate to fill a vacancy caused by death and took his seat May 26, 1890, and served until February 4, 1893, when he resigned to accept a Cabinet portfolio; Secretary of the Treasury, 1893–97; moved to New York City and resumed the practice of law; died in New York City July 31, 1910.

Fifty–first Congress

THOMAS BRACKETT REED (Republican), born in Portland, Maine, October 18, 1839; attended the public schools; was graduated from Bowdoin College, Brunswick, Maine, in 1860; studied law; acting assistant paymaster, U.S. Navy, from April 19, 1864, to November 4, 1865; was admitted to the bar in 1865 and commenced practice in Portland; member of the state house of representatives, 1868–69; served in the state senate in 1870; attorney general of Maine, 1870–72; city solicitor of Portland, 1874–77; elected as a Republican to the Forty-fifth and to the eleven succeeding Congresses and served from March 4, 1877, to September 4, 1899, when he resigned; served as Speaker of the House in the Fifty-first, Fifty-fourth, and Fifty-fifth Congresses; moved to New York City and practiced law; died in Washington, D.C., December 7, 1902.

Fifty–second and Fifty–third Congresses

CHARLES FREDERICK CRISP (Democrat), born in Sheffield, England, January 29, 1845; later in that year his parents immigrated to the United States and settled in Georgia; attended the common schools of Savannah and Macon, Ga.; during the Civil War entered the Confederate Army in May 1861; commissioned lieutenant in Company K, Tenth Regiment, Virginia Infantry, and served with that regiment until May 12, 1864, when he became a prisoner of war; upon his release from Fort Delaware in June 1865 joined his parents at Ellaville, Schley County, Ga.; studied law at Americus, Ga.; was admitted to the bar in 1866 and commenced practice at Ellaville; appointed solicitor-general of the southwestern judicial circuit in 1872 and reappointed in 1873 for a term of four years; appointed judge of the superior court of the same circuit in June 1877; elected by the general assembly to the same office in 1878; re-elected judge for a term of four years in 1880; resigned that office in September 1882 to accept the Democratic nomination for Congress; permanent president of the Democratic convention which assembled at Atlanta in April 1883 to nominate a candidate for governor; elected as a Democrat to the Forty-eighth and to the six succeeding Congresses and served from March 4, 1883, until his death; was Speaker of the House in the Fifty-second and Fifty-third Congresses; nominated for U.S. Senator in the state primary of 1896; died in Atlanta, Ga., October 23, 1896.

Fifty–fourth and Fifty–fifth Congresses

THOMAS B. REED. *See* Fifty-first Congress

Fifty–sixth and Fifty–seventh Congresses

DAVID BREMNER HENDERSON (Republican), born in Old Deer, Scotland, March 14, 1840; immigrated to the United States with his parents, who settled in Winnebago County, Ill., in 1846; moved to Fayette County, Iowa, in 1849; attended the common schools and the Upper Iowa University at Fayette; during the Civil War enlisted in the Union Army September 15, 1861, as a private in Company C, Twelfth Regiment, Iowa Volunteer Infantry; was elected and commissioned first lieutenant of that company and served with it until discharged, owing to the loss of a leg February 26, 1863; commissioner of the board of enrollment of the third district of Iowa from May 1863 to June 1864; entered the Army as colonel of the Forty-sixth Regiment, Iowa Volunteer Infantry, and served until the close of the war; studied law; was admitted to the bar in 1865 and commenced practice in Dubuque, Iowa; collector of internal revenue for the third district of Iowa from November 1865 until June 1869, when he resigned; assistant U.S. district attorney for the northern district of Iowa, 1869–71; elected as a Republican to the Forty-eighth and to the nine succeeding Congresses (March 4, 1883, to March 3, 1903); declined to be a candidate for renomination in 1902; served as Speaker of the House in the Fifty-sixth and Fifty-seventh Congresses; died in Dubuque, Iowa, February 25, 1906.

Fifty–eighth, Fifty–ninth, Sixtieth, and Sixty–first Congresses

JOSEPH GURNEY CANNON (Republican), born in Guilford, Guilford County, N.C., May 7, 1836; moved with his parents to Bloomingdale, Ind., in 1840; completed preparatory studies; studied law at the Cincinnati Law School; was admitted to the bar in 1858 and commenced practice in Terre Haute, Ind., the same year; moved to Tuscola, Ill., in 1859; state's attorney for the twenty-seventh judicial district of Illinois from March 1861 to December 1868; elected as a Republican to the Forty-third and to the eight succeeding Congresses (March 4, 1873, to March 3, 1891); moved to Danville, Ill., in 1878; unsuccessful candidate for re-election in 1890 to the Fifty-second Congress; elected to the Fifty-third and to the nine succeeding Congresses (March 4, 1893, to March 3, 1913); served as Speaker of the House in the Fifty-eighth, Fifty-ninth, Sixtieth, and Sixty-first Congresses; received fifty-eight votes for the presidential nomination at the Republican National Convention at Chicago in 1908; unsuccessful candidate for re-election in 1912 to the Sixty-third Congress; again elected to the Sixty-fourth and to the three succeeding Congresses (March 4, 1915, to March 3, 1923); declined renomination at the end of the Sixty-seventh Congress; retired from public life; died in Danville, Ill., November 12, 1926.

Sixty–second, Sixty–third, Sixty–fourth, and Sixty–fifth Congresses

JAMES BEAUCHAMP (CHAMP) CLARK (Democrat), born near Lawrenceburg, Anderson County, Ky., March 7, 1850; attended the common schools and Kentucky University at Lexington; was graduated from Bethany (W. Va.) College in 1873 and from Cincinnati Law School in 1875; president of Marshall College, Huntington, W. Va., 1873–74; admitted to the bar in 1875; edited a country newspaper and practiced law; moved to Bowling Green, Pike County, Mo., in 1876; city attorney of Louisiana, Mo., and Bowling Green, Mo., 1878–81; presidential elector on the Democratic ticket in 1880; deputy prosecuting attorney and prosecuting attorney of Pike County, 1885–89; member of the state house of representatives in 1889 and 1891; delegate to the Trans-Mississippi Congress at Denver in May 1891; elected as a Democrat to the Fifty-third Congress (March 4, 1893, to March 3, 1895); unsuccessful candidate for re-election in 1894 to the Fifty-fourth Congress; elected to the Fifty-fifth and the eleven succeeding Congresses and served from March 4, 1897, until his death; Democratic minority leader of the House in the Sixtieth and Sixty-first Congresses and served as Speaker of the House in the Sixty-second, Sixty-third, Sixty-fourth, and Sixty-fifth Congresses; chairman of the Democratic National Convention at St. Louis in 1904; was the leading candidate in the Baltimore Democratic National Convention of 1912 for the presidential nomination on twenty-nine ballots, and had a clear majority on eight; died in Washington, D.C., on March 2, 1921.

Sixty–sixth, Sixty–seventh, and Sixty–eighth Congresses

FREDERICK HUNTINGTON GILLETT (Republican), born in Westfield, Hampden County, Mass., October 16, 1851; attended the public schools; was graduated from Amherst College, Amherst, Mass., in 1874 and from the law department of

Harvard University in 1877; was admitted to the bar at Springfield, Mass., in 1877 and commenced practice in that city; assistant attorney-general of Massachusetts, 1879–82; member of the state house of representatives, 1890–91; elected as a Republican to the Fifty-third and to the fifteen succeeding Congresses, thus serving from March 4, 1893, to March 3, 1925; Speaker in the Sixty-sixth, Sixty-seventh, and Sixty-eighth Congresses; was not a candidate for renomination to the Sixty-ninth Congress, having become a candidate of the Republican party for U.S. Senator; elected to the Senate in 1924 and served from March 4, 1925, to March 3, 1931; was not a candidate for renomination in 1930; engaged in literary pursuits; died in Springfield, Mass., July 31, 1935.

Sixty–ninth, Seventieth, and Seventy–first Congresses

NICHOLAS LONGWORTH (Republican), born in Cincinnati, Ohio, November 5, 1869; attended the Franklin School in Cincinnati, and was graduated from Harvard University in 1891; spent one year at Harvard Law School, and was graduated from the Cincinnati Law School in 1894; was admitted to the bar in 1894 and commenced practice in Cincinnati; member of the board of education of Cincinnati in 1898; member of the state house of representatives, 1899–1900; served in the state senate, 1901–03; elected as a Republican to the Fifty-eighth and to the four succeeding Congresses (March 4, 1903, to March 3, 1913); unsuccessful candidate for re-election in 1912 to the Sixty-third Congress; elected to the Sixty-fourth and to the eight succeeding Congresses and served from March 4, 1915, until his death; Republican majority floor leader during the Sixty-eighth Congress; Speaker of the House during the Sixty-ninth, Seventieth, and Seventy-first Congresses; died in Aiken, S.C., while on a visit, April 9, 1931.

Seventy–second Congress

JOHN NANCE GARNER (Democrat), born near Detroit, Red River County, Texas, November 22, 1868; had limited elementary education; studied law in Clarksville, Texas; was admitted to the bar in 1890 and commenced practice in Uvalde, Texas; judge of Uvalde County, 1893–96; member of the state house of representatives, 1898–1902; delegate to the Democratic National Conventions in 1900, 1916, and 1924; elected as a Democrat to the Fifty-eighth and to the fourteen succeeding Congresses (March 4, 1903, to March 3, 1933); served as minority floor leader in the Seventy-first Congress and as Speaker in the Seventy-second Congress; re-elected to the Seventy-third Congress on November 8, 1932, and on the same day was elected Vice-President of the United States on the ticket headed by Franklin D. Roosevelt; resigned from the Seventy-third Congress March 3, 1933; re-elected Vice-President in 1936, thus serving in that office from March 4, 1933, to January 20, 1941; retired to private life in 1941.

Seventy–third Congress

HENRY THOMAS RAINEY (Democrat), born in Carrollton, Greene County, Ill., August 20, 1860; attended the public schools and Knox Academy and Knox College, Galesburg, Ill.; was graduated from Amherst (Mass.) College in 1883 and from the Union College of Law, Chicago, in 1885; was admitted to the bar in 1885 and commenced practice in Carrollton; master in chancery for Greene County from 1887 to 1895, when he resigned; elected as a Democrat to the Fifty-eighth and to the eight succeeding Congresses (March 4, 1903, to March 3, 1921); unsuccessfully contested the election of Guy L. Shaw to the Sixty-seventh Congress; engaged in agricultural pursuits; elected to the Sixty-eighth and to the five succeeding Congresses and served from March 4, 1923, until his death; elected Speaker in the Seventy-third Congress on March 9, 1933, and served until his death in a hospital in St. Louis, Mo., August 19, 1934.

Seventy–fourth Congress

JOSEPH WELLINGTON BYRNS (Democrat), born near Cedar Hill, Robertson County, Tenn., July 20, 1869; attended the common schools; was graduated from Nashville High School in 1887 and from the law department of Vanderbilt University, Nashville, in 1890; was admitted to the bar in 1890 and commenced the practice of law in Nashville; member of the state house of representatives in 1895, 1897, and again in 1899, serving as speaker during the last term; member of the state senate in 1901; unsuccessful candidate for district attorney of Davidson County in 1902; presidential elector on the Democratic ticket in 1904; elected as a Democrat to the Sixty-first and to the thirteen succeeding Congresses and served from March 4, 1909, until his death; was a nominee for re-election to the Seventy-fifth Congress at the time of his death; chairman of the Democratic National Congressional Campaign Committee, 1928–30; served as Democratic majority leader during the Seventy-third Congress and as Speaker of the House during the Seventy-fourth Congress; died in Washington, D.C., June 4, 1936.

WILLIAM BROCKMAN BANKHEAD (Democrat), born in Moscow, Lamar County, Ala., April 12, 1874; attended the county schools; was graduated from the University of Alabama at Tuscaloosa in 1893 and from the Georgetown University Law School, Washington, D.C., in 1895; was admitted to the bar the same year and commenced practice in Huntsville, Ala.; city attorney of Huntsville, 1898–1902; member of the state house of representatives, 1900–01; moved to Jasper, Walker County, Ala., in 1905 and continued the practice of law; solicitor of the fourteenth judicial circuit of Alabama, 1910–14; elected as a Democrat to the Sixty-fifth and to the eleven succeeding Congresses and served from March 4, 1917, until his death; elected Democratic majority leader of the House in the Seventy-fourth Congress; elected Speaker during the Seventy-fourth Congress and served until his death; delegate to the Democratic National Convention at Chicago in 1940; died in Washington, D.C., September 15, 1940.

Seventy–fifth Congress

WILLIAM B. BANKHEAD. *See* Seventy-fourth Congress

Seventy–sixth Congress

WILLIAM B. BANKHEAD. *See* Seventy-fourth Congress

SAM (Samuel Taliafero) RAYBURN (Democrat), born near Kingston, Roane County, Tenn., January 6, 1882; moved to Fannin County, Texas, in 1887 with his parents, who settled near Windom; attended the rural schools and was graduated from the East Texas Normal College, Commerce, Texas, in 1902; studied law at the University of Texas in Austin; was admitted to the bar in 1908 and commenced practice in Bonham, Fannin County; member of the state house of representatives, 1907–13, and served as speaker during the last two years; elected as a Democrat to the Sixty-third and to the twenty-four succeeding Congresses and served from March 4, 1913, until his death; majority leader in the Seventy-fifth and Seventy-sixth Congresses; minority leader in the Eightieth and Eighty-third Congresses; elected Speaker September 16, 1940, in the Seventy-sixth Congress to fill the vacancy caused by the death of Speaker William B. Bankhead; re-elected Speaker in the Seventy-seventh, Seventy-eighth, Seventy-ninth, Eighty-first, Eighty-second, Eighty-fourth, Eighty-fifth, Eighty-sixth, and Eighty-seventh Congresses; died in Bonham, Texas, November 16, 1961.

Seventy–seventh, Seventy–eighth, and Seventy–ninth Congresses

SAM RAYBURN. *See* Seventy-sixth Congress

Eightieth Congress

JOSEPH WILLIAM MARTIN, JR. (Republican), born in North Attleboro, Bristol County, Mass., November 3, 1884; attended the public schools, and was graduated from North Attleboro High School in 1902; reporter on the Attleboro *Sun* and Providence *Journal*, 1902–08; publisher of the *Evening Chronicle* at North Attleboro from 1908 and also publisher of the Franklin (Mass.) *Sentinel*; member of the state house of representatives, 1912–14; served in the state senate, 1914–17; chairman of the Massachusetts Street Railway Investigating Commission in 1917; chairman of the Massachusetts legislative campaign committee in 1917; presidential elector on the Republican ticket of Harding and Coolidge in 1920; executive secretary of the Republican state committee, 1922–25; delegate to the Republican National Conventions in 1916, 1936, 1940, 1948, 1952, and 1956; permanent chairman of the Republican National Conventions in 1940, 1944, 1948, 1952, 1956, and 1960; member of the Republican National Committee, serving as chairman, 1940–42; elected as a Republican to the Sixty-ninth and to the succeeding nineteen Congresses; elected minority leader Seventy-sixth to Eighty-fifth Congresses except the Eightieth and Eighty-third, in which he was elected Speaker.

Eighty–first and Eighty–second Congresses

SAM RAYBURN. *See* Seventy-sixth Congress

Eighty–third Congress

JOSEPH W. MARTIN. *See* Eightieth Congress

Eighty–fourth, Eighty–fifth, Eighty–sixth, and Eighty–seventh Congresses

SAM RAYBURN. *See* Seventy-sixth Congress

JOHN WILLIAM McCORMACK (Democrat), born in Boston, Mass., December 21, 1891; attended the public schools; studied law in a private law office; was admitted to the bar in 1913 and began practice in Boston; member of the state constitutional convention, 1917–18; during the First World War served in the United States Army, 1917–18; served in the state house of representatives, 1920–22; member of the state senate, 1923–26, serving as Democratic floor leader, 1925–26; delegate to all Democratic state conventions since 1920; delegate to the Democratic National Conventions in 1932, 1940, 1944, and 1948; elected as a Democrat to the Seventieth Congress to fill a vacancy caused by death and on the same day was elected to the Seventy-first Congress; re-elected to the Seventy-second and to the sixteen succeeding Congresses, with service dating from November 6, 1928; majority floor leader from September 16, 1940, to January 3, 1947; from January 3, 1949, to January 3, 1953; and from January 3, 1955, until his election as Speaker, second session, Eighty-seventh Congress; re-elected Speaker of the House in the Eighty-eighth Congress.

Eighty–eighth Congress

JOHN W. McCORMACK. *See* Eighty-seventh Congress

BIBLIOGRAPHY

ANGLE, PAUL M. *Crossroads: 1913.* New York: Rand McNally & Company, 1963.

BARRY, DAVID S. *Forty Years in Washington.* Boston: Little, Brown & Company, 1924.

BATES, ERNEST SUTHERLAND. *The Story of Congress, 1879–1935.* New York: Harper & Brothers, 1936.

BELL, JACK. *The Splendid Misery.* New York: Doubleday & Company, 1960.

Biographical Directory of the American Congress, 1774–1961. Washington, D.C.: Government Printing Office, 1961.

BOLLES, BLAIR. *Tryant From Illinois: Uncle Joe Cannon's Experiment with Personal Power.* New York: Norton, 1951.

BOWERS, CLAUDE G. *Beveridge and the Progressive Era.* Boston: Houghton Mifflin Company, 1932.

BRADFORD, GAMALIEL. *As God Made Them—Portraits of Some 19th Century Americans.* Boston: Houghton Mifflin Company, 1929.

BROWN, GEORGE R. *The Leadership of Congress.* Indianapolis: Bobbs-Merrill Company, 1922.

BROWN, JOHN MASON. *Through These Men.* New York: Harper & Brothers, 1956.

BUSBEY, L. WHITE. *Uncle Joe Cannon: The Story of a Pioneer American.* New York: Henry Holt, 1927.

CARPENTER, FRANK G. *Carp's Washington.* New York: McGraw-Hill Book Company, 1960.

CARTER, EDWARD W., and CHARLES C. ROHLFING. *The American Government and Its Work.* New York: Macmillan Company, 1952.

CHA'NG-WEI, CH'IU. *The Speaker of the House of Representatives.* New York: Columbia University Press, 1928.

CLARK, CHAMP. *My Quarter Century of American Politics.* New York: Harper & Brothers, 1920.

DEPEW, CHAUNCEY M. *My Memories of Eighty Years.* New York: Charles Scribner's Sons, 1923.

DINGLEY, EDWARD NELSON. *The Life and Times of Nelson Dingley, Jr.* Kalamazoo, Mich.: Ihling Bros. & Everard, 1902.

DOROUGH, C. DWIGHT. *Mr. Sam.* New York: Random House, 1962.

Encyclopædia Britannica. Chicago: Encyclopædia Britannica, Inc., 1961.

FARLEY, JAMES A. *Behind the Ballots, the Personal History of a Politician.* New York: Harcourt, Brace & Company, 1938.

FOLLETT, M. P. *The Speaker of the House of Representatives.* New York: Longmans, Green & Company, 1896.

FULLER, HUBERT BRUCE. *The Speakers of the House.* Boston: Little, Brown & Company, 1909.

GALLOWAY, GEORGE B. *Congress at the Crossroads.* New York: Thomas Y. Crowell Company, 1946.

———. *History of the United States House of Representatives.* New York: Thomas Y. Crowell Company, 1961.

GWINN, WILLIAM R. *Uncle Joe Cannon, Archfoe of Insurgency: A History of the Rise and Fall of Cannonism.* New York: Bookman Associates, 1957.

HAWORTH, PAUL LELAND. *The Hayes-Tilden Election.* Cleveland: Burrows Brothers, 1906.

HULL, CORDELL. *The Memoirs of Cordell Hull.* 2 vols. New York: Macmillan Company, 1948.

JAMES, MARQUIS. *Mr. Garner of Texas.* Indianapolis: Bobbs-Merrill Company, 1939.

JOSEPHSON, MATTHEW. *The Politicos, 1865–1896.* New York: Harcourt, Brace & Company, 1938.

LUCE, ROBERT. *Congress: An Explanation.* Cambridge, Mass.: Harvard University Press, 1926.

LYNES, RUSSELL. *The Domesticated Americans*. New York: Harper & Row, 1962.

McCALL, SAMUEL E. *The Life of Thomas Brackett Reed*. Boston: Houghton Mifflin Company, 1914.

MacNEIL, NEIL. *Forge of Democracy*. New York: David McKay Company, 1963.

MARTIN, JOE (as told to ROBERT DONAVAN). *My First Fifty Years in Politics*. New York: McGraw-Hill Book Company, 1960.

NEUBERGER, RICHARD L., and STEPHEN B. KAHN. *Integrity, the Life of George W. Norris*. New York: Vanguard Press, 1937.

PRINGLE, HENRY F. *The Life and Times of William Howard Taft*. 2 vols. New York: Farrar & Rinehart, 1939.

ROBINSON, WILLIAM A. *Thomas B. Reed, Parliamentarian*. New York: Dodd, Mead & Company, 1930.

SALTER, J. T. *Public Men In and Out of Office*. Chapel Hill, N.C.: University of North Carolina Press, 1946.

SCHLESINGER, ARTHUR M., JR. *The Age of Jackson*. Boston: Little, Brown & Company, 1946.

SMITH, WILLIAM HENRY. *Speakers of the House of Representatives of the United States*. Baltimore: Simon J. Gaeng, 1928.

STIMPSON, GEORGE W. *A Book About Politics*. New York: Harper & Brothers, 1952.

STONE, MELVILLE E. *Fifty Years a Journalist*. Garden City, New York: Doubleday, Page & Company, 1921.

SULLIVAN, MARK. *Our Times*. 6 vols. New York: Charles Scribner's Sons, 1926–35.

TIMMONS, BASCOM N. *Garner of Texas*. New York: Harper & Brothers, 1948.

TROLLOPE, MRS. FRANCES. *Domestic Manners of the Americans*. New York: Alfred A. Knopf, 1949.

TRUMAN, HARRY S. *Year of Decisions*. New York: Doubleday & Company, 1955.

WEINBURG, ARTHUR and LILA (eds.). *The Muckrakers*. New York: Simon and Schuster, 1961.

WHITE, WILLIAM ALLEN. *The Autobiography of William Allen White*. New York: Macmillan Company, 1928.

Index

ABOUT THE AUTHOR

Booth Mooney, formerly executive assistant to then Senator Lyndon B. Johnson, is a Texan. He is the author of *The Lyndon Johnson Story,* which was widely received as a warm, human portrait of the President.

Mr. Mooney was born on a Texas farm in 1912. He was seventeen when he went into newspaper work, and his interest in politics was stimulated in these early years when he was covering the county courthouse. For the next eighteen years he worked as a reporter on various newspapers in the region. At the outbreak of World War II he was associate editor of a Dallas magazine devoted to economics and government.

After three years in the Army Air Corps, he started and operated his own public relations firm until, in 1953, Senator Johnson asked him to join his staff. Since 1958 he has been a public relations consultant and free lance writer in Washington, D.C.

The inspiration to write MR. SPEAKER came from the late Senator Sam Rayburn, whose friendship Booth Mooney valued and whom he admired not merely as a fellow Texan but as a man dedicated to government and politics as "the arts of the possible."

Mr. Mooney is married. He lives with his family, which includes a young son and a daughter, in the Maryland suburbs of the capital.